Oracy

Oracy

The Transformative Power of Finding Your Voice

NEIL MERCER

THE BODLEY HEAD
LONDON

1 3 5 7 9 10 8 6 4 2

The Bodley Head, an imprint of Vintage, is part of the
Penguin Random House group of companies

Vintage, Penguin Random House UK, One Embassy Gardens,
8 Viaduct Gardens, London SW11 7BW

penguin.co.uk/vintage
global.penguinrandomhouse.com

First published by The Bodley Head in 2025

Typeset in 13.5/16pt Garamond MT Std by Jouve (UK), Milton Keynes
Printed and bound in Great Britain by Clays Ltd, Elcograf S.p.A.

The authorised representative in the EEA is Penguin Random House Ireland,
Morrison Chambers, 32 Nassau Street, Dublin D02 YH68

A CIP catalogue record for this book is available from the British Library

ISBN 9781847928566

Penguin Random House is committed to a sustainable future
for our business, our readers and our planet. This book is made
from Forest Stewardship Council® certified paper.

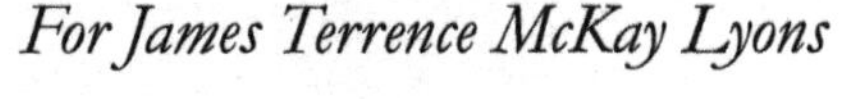

For James Terrence McKay Lyons

Contents

Acknowledgements

When I was writing this book, the constructively critical comments of my Bodley Head editor Alice Skinner and my wife Lyn Dawes were, at every stage, vital sources of support and encouragement. I am also very grateful to my Oracy Cambridge colleague Topsy Page for her feedback and advice on draft chapters, and I thank all the other members of the Oracy Cambridge team – Ayesha Ahmed, Pete Dudley, Alan Howe, Wendy Lee, James Mannion, Neil Phillipson, Benjamin Strawbridge, Paul Warwick and Rupert Wegerif – for their brilliant contributions to the interthinking process which has informed everything I have written. It was a privilege to work with Faculty of Education colleagues, and particularly Sara Hennessy and Christine Howe, on the research I describe in Chapter 7. My agent Jim Gill gave me the kind of encouragement and help I needed to write this book; and the contributions of Rowena Skelton-Wallace, James Nightingale, John Garrett and Alex Bell were all vital for achieving the final version. My college Hughes Hall, University of Cambridge, has provided exactly the kind of institutional support needed to make Oracy Cambridge come to life. In the wider world, warm collaborative relationships with members of Voice 21 have been very important in helping me make practical sense of complex issues, as have links with schools, teachers and other organisations involved with oracy.

Introduction

Imagine this: you have been invited to speak to an audience on a topic about which you are passionate. How does this make you feel? Does it fill you with dread, or spark just the right kind of motivation to start preparing your speech? Or imagine this: you have been asked to join a series of committee meetings, with people you do not know, to come up with a solution to an issue facing your local community. Again, do you feel daunted or enthusiastic? Do you know how to make such meetings productive and enjoyable? Your reaction to either scenario may be influenced by whether you are a shy or confident person. But how well you handle these situations in practice, and how well you feel you can do so, will be dependent on your spoken language skills.

In its routine, spontaneous forms, talk can seem rather insubstantial – something not to be pondered over, reconsidered, reviewed and analysed in the ways we might with written text. We sometimes compare it unfavourably to action – 'It's only words', as the Bee Gees tell us. Yet talking is one of the main ways we relate to each other as human beings. Spoken language can solemnise a marriage or break someone's heart; words can be used to declare war or offer peace; they can pronounce someone guilty or innocent. And whether or not someone is found guilty can be determined by what is said, and what listeners make of what they hear.

Until we learn to read and write with any facility, which may take our first nine or ten years, most of us are reliant on spoken language for expressing our thoughts and discovering what others think. It enables us to justify and explain who we are and what we do. Although the written word may become part of our work and social lives, we still want to talk, to keep conversations alive: we arrange a 'catch up' meeting with friends, we visit mum and dad, attend an interview, consult a doctor, take a meeting, discuss with a mechanic what's wrong with our car.

In Chapter 1, I will trace how the emergence of language in our evolutionary history is bound up with our distinctively social intelligence. But spoken language is not hardwired. It is a toolkit: we have to learn how to use it in different ways, in different situations, to achieve many different things. We can build or destroy relationships, gain or lose opportunities, solve problems or compound them. And as with any toolkit, we need to become skilled in its use. In Chapter 2, I will discuss the crucial role parents, teachers and others responsible for caring for children can play in that education process. In Chapter 3, I will describe the full range of oracy skills. The language we use is an important component of our identity, as I show in Chapter 4. It is primarily through talking with others that we become part of a community and gain access to its culture.

At school, I learned how to calculate the area of a triangle, but not how to make a good speech, chair a meeting or work well in a team. Today, young people all over the world are taught how to read and write, and manipulate numbers, but the fact still remains that few are taught how to talk. And even fewer will be taught anything *about* talk – its nature and form, its cultural roots and how it differs from written language.

Throughout our lives, we will encounter people using talk to try to persuade, control and even deliberately mislead us – so it is vital that we understand how this can be done. In schools and universities, students are commonly encouraged to become critical readers: guidance is widely available on developing these skills. But students are rarely encouraged, or helped, to become critical listeners.

Of course, a good education should help young people develop a broad range of skills, and I would never suggest that learning maths is not important. Who knows what each of us will need as we progress in life? But the low priority given in most education systems to understanding and teaching spoken language is hard to justify. To steal a metaphor from the novelist E. M. Forster: for most of us, using spoken language is a public performance on the violin, in which you have to learn the instrument as you go along. This doesn't have to be the case.

I have often asked a lecture theatre of new students who are enrolled on our course to become primary school teachers how many of them had any kind of talk tuition in school. If there are sixty there, then about ten will put their hands up – and they will invariably have gone to private schools. Yet, since the ancient Greeks, we've known how to teach the skills needed to speak well in public, as I will explain in Chapter 5.

By learning to speak and listen we acquire much more than an ability to share information: we become able to think creatively and constructively with others. Most significant human achievements have not been made by individuals; they have been achieved through collective thought and action. But, as history also tells us – and we all will know from personal experience – collective endeavour is not a foolproof process. We have to learn how to collaborate well – and in Chapter 6 I will explain what this involves. We do not need to discover how to do so by trial and error: we can be taught the relevant skills.

Tony Blair, who is famous for his oratory skills, once said his government's priorities were 'education, education, education'. Nowhere is the effective use of talk more important than in school. Talk makes classroom education happen; and how well it is used can make all the difference to the results. The best teachers use talk as a professional toolkit in the classroom, as I will describe in Chapter 7. Speaking and listening can also promote students' learning and their individual development as thinkers and problem-solvers.

When people first encounter the concept of oracy, and discover that it concerns the development of spoken language skills, they often assume that it essentially means teaching public speaking. This is not so surprising, given that an 'orator' is a speech maker. 'You want more debating in state schools,' journalists say. While that would be a good idea, it is not the whole truth. I certainly want more young people to become effective communicators, but not just on a stage. I want them to learn how to collaborate in groups and meetings, and to become successful at using talk in many ways to get things done.

Andrew Wilkinson, professor of education at the University of Birmingham in the 1960s, invented the word 'oracy'.[1] He was one of the first to highlight the lack of attention given to spoken language in education policy and practice. Along with other pioneers like James Britton, Douglas Barnes, Joan Tough and Harold Rosen, he made it his mission to strive for change. Part of the challenge, he suggested, was that we lacked a clear and precise term, an equivalent to 'literacy' and 'numeracy'. 'Talk' sounds rather inconsequential, and the only other option was to resort to clumsy phrases such as 'oral communication skills'. So he came up with his new word. Wilkinson's definition of oracy was straightforward: 'the ability to use the oral skills of speaking and listening'.

Since then, other definitions have been proposed. One of the worst, I am ashamed to say, is associated with my own university. The *Cambridge English Dictionary* defines oracy as 'the ability to speak clearly and grammatically correctly'. There is nothing there about listening or communicating, and apparently what matters most is that your grammar is perfect. Let's leave that one behind. In contrast, the leading British oracy charity, Voice 21, has expanded Wilkinson's definition: 'oracy is the ability to articulate ideas, develop understanding and engage with others through spoken language'.[2] The Commission on the Future of Oracy in England, which published its report in 2024, defined oracy as: 'Articulating ideas, developing understanding and engaging with others through speaking, listening and communication.'[3] The Commission added 'communication' to be inclusive and acknowledge the importance of non-verbal communication, as well as to avoid marginalising forms such as sign language. Sign language is a vital form of communication with its own international and regional varieties. I agree that its importance and richness deserve to be fully recognised, but the skills required for using it well are not oracy skills. We also communicate through the written word, through pictures, through dance and through music, none of which should be subsumed under oracy. Unless we set boundaries on a concept, I think it is difficult to bring it into focus. The definition my Oracy Cambridge colleagues have settled on is: 'the ability to use the skills of speaking, listening and non-verbal communication for a wide range of purposes'.

I firmly believe that the development of oracy skills needs to be underpinned by an awareness and understanding of the nature of spoken language and how it functions in human life. For example, oracy education can help students understand why they, as a speaker, may experience or exercise prejudice when they interact with someone who speaks differently. To provide a suitable foundation for oracy education, we need to go beyond simple definitions, and think of oracy as having three aspects: 'learning how to talk', 'learning through talk' and 'learning about talk':

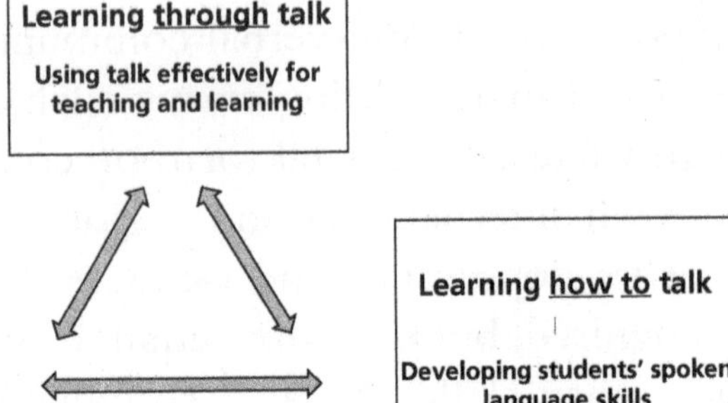

'Learning how to talk' is about becoming able to communicate effectively through spoken language. 'Learning about talk' means understanding language in its social, political and cultural context. The third aspect, 'Learning through talk', is how to use spoken language for teaching and learning. Combined, they represent vital components of what should be taught in schools: oracy as both a skill set and a curriculum subject.

'The support, in 2024, of the Commission on the Future of Oracy in England for this three-aspect model was very welcome – as was its conclusion that oracy is just as foundational for children's learning as reading, writing and arithmetic and so should be part of children's educational entitlement throughout the school years. At the time of writing, the British government has set up a review of the national curriculum for England and Wales. My hope is that it will locate *learning about* talk firmly within the English curriculum. It is in English lessons that students already learn about the grammar, history and genres of written language, so it would make sense for them also to learn there about the structure, forms and uses of spoken language: how it is shaped by place and culture, and how it changes over time. 'Learning how to talk' would also naturally come under English, alongside other language skills involved in reading, writing and spelling. Some oracy skills, such as voice projection and pacing, are already often taught in drama lessons. As with literacy, oracy skills can also be developed through the teaching of other curriculum subjects. And 'Learning through talk' must be a cross-curricular concern. The effective use of spoken language, by both teachers and students, is essential for learning every subject, from maths, history and science to art and geography. For these reasons, all teachers should be oracy teachers.

It is largely forgotten that there was once a National Oracy Project, which ran from 1988 to 1993, and which involved most local education authorities in England and Wales. Many schools joined enthusiastically in pursuing its aims of making young people's voices heard in the classroom, of celebrating oral activities such as storytelling and of sharing knowledge about diverse spoken language communities. However, a re-elected Conservative government saw oracy as a distraction from the important business of teaching what they considered 'the basics' – or the three R's – and so the project's achievements and legacy were dismissed. I was actively involved in that project, and although many of us continued to keep the oracy flame alight, we did so in a far less supportive political environment. For more than a decade, the term 'oracy' almost went out of use.

Things started to change around 2012 when School 21, the first state-funded school to provide regular oracy lessons, was established in east London[4]. Shortly afterwards, the Education Endowment Foundation funded the joint efforts of School 21 and the University of Cambridge to create the first ever representation of spoken language skills, the Oracy Skills Framework. In 2015, two organisations were set up with the express purpose of promoting oracy and providing the relevant professional development for teachers: Voice 21 and Oracy Cambridge. Once workshops became available and conferences were advertised, strong interest was immediately apparent. Other UK charities, such as the English-Speaking Union, the National Literacy Trust and Speech and Language UK, have also made oracy a more explicit part of their mission.

In the wider world, a group of Japanese teachers have set up an Oracy Japan collective, supported by Teikyo University. Schools in the Norwegian municipalities of Sandnes and Klepp are developing an oracy curriculum and training their teachers accordingly. The University of South Australia now collaborates with Oracy Cambridge, and our work has informed the new Kazakhstan school curriculum. Northeast Normal University, China, which is responsible for national teacher development policy, is creating resources for oracy. And in 2024, teachers of English from thirty-four countries came to a conference in Cambridge to find out how to develop their students' oracy skills.

Policymakers are now recognising the importance of oracy too. The European Union hosted a 'Speaking Citizens' event on oracy in 2024. The Welsh government has added an oracy strand to its bilingual national curriculum, and Education Scotland has supported our recent oracy initiatives. The glaring anomaly was England's Conservative government, which would not even sanction the official use of the term oracy. But as I write, the first Labour government for fourteen years has come into office, with an election promise from the new prime minister, Sir Keir Starmer: 'Let's raise the importance of speaking skills – "oracy" as academics call it. Because these skills are absolutely critical for our children's future success . . . Labour in government will work to weave oracy through the curriculum at all stages, so that every young person leaves school with the confidence and skills to use their voice to overcome barriers and make the most of their lives.'[5]

There is increasing recognition, then, that being an effective communicator is an essential component of the 'twenty-first-century skills' that young people should gain from their education. But of course, there are still the detractors. In 2023, the TV presenter Jeremy Clarkson, an authority on fast cars and running a novelty farm, wrote in *The Times* that: 'Teaching thick kids oracy is like teaching a tortoise how to make a coffee table and teaching bright kids how to speak is pointless as well, because they're bright, so it comes naturally.'[6] Clarkson has also boasted about failing his A levels, so I wonder which kind of kid he thinks he was. He was educated at Malvern College, an expensive public school. Such schools have fostered public-speaking and debating skills for years, while most state-funded schools in the UK have not. The conspiratorial explanation for why wealthy, right-wing provocateurs like Clarkson oppose oracy education is, of course, that they want to keep it just for the children of the upper middle classes. Make oracy education more widely available and anyone might feel they could become a TV presenter, a High Court judge or politician.

From a very different political perspective, the linguist Deborah Cameron has also criticised recent oracy initiatives.[7] She has argued that they sustain a narrow and prejudicial definition of what constitutes 'speaking well'. I recognise her concern that oracy could be hijacked by people who wish to impose an inappropriate and ill-informed conception of 'correct English'. Those of us actively involved with oracy are acutely aware of such dangers – and I give them due attention in Chapter 4. It is important to challenge foolish imperatives such as 'students should always speak to teachers in full sentences', and reject the notion that young people should all be encouraged to sound like middle-class, southern English speakers. Prejudiced attitudes to 'nonstandard' varieties of English need to be opposed. Rather than bolstering misguided attempts to 'police' young people's language, I believe that oracy education can contribute to the fight against discrimination and social disadvantage.

In fact, there is a long tradition of 'grass roots' oracy in Britain, linked to campaigns for universal suffrage, the establishment of unions and battles for gender equality.[8] Such activities were common in British cities, towns and villages in the nineteenth and early twentieth centuries, as working-class people developed their speaking and listening skills by setting up discussion groups, public recitations, classes, summer camps and drama clubs. There are organisations today that offer training in public speaking to less privileged young people.[9] But in the wake of the decline of many such initiatives, it must be schools that take on the mantle.

Like any powerful notion which rises up the public agenda, oracy can be misunderstood and wilfully misrepresented.

Oracy is not just about public oratory: it is about collaborating, actively listening, thinking collectively, teaching and learning. It is not about constraining young people's use of language, or directing them along a single, restrictive, linguistic path. Oracy is about expanding and developing young people's language repertoires, empowering them by giving them the skills to handle a whole range of communication situations. It is about helping them to appreciate how talk is used and to understand how it relates to social structures and attitudes. I want to convince you that oracy matters, and I hope this book gives you the ammunition to convince others too.

1. Talking Ourselves Up

It might seem strange in a book about oracy to begin by talking about the evolution of our species. But the evolution of spoken language has a close relationship to the way we think. It seems that the first true humans emerged about 200,000 years ago. How did we become – for better or worse – the dominant creatures on the planet? It certainly wasn't because we were the strongest. It wasn't even due to our ancestors, as individuals, being the most ingenious animals at solving problems. It was because we became able to think together.

Other creatures can co-ordinate their actions and work collectively, in complex ways, to ensure their mutual survival. Honeybees are a good example. After going off to find sources of nectar in their vicinity, individual bees come back to the hive and tell their fellow workers precisely where those food sources can be found by performing their distinctive 'waggle dance'. These movements are sometimes called the language of bees. However, at the end of a working day, when the nectar gathering is complete, the queen bee cannot say: 'Well, things didn't go well today – we are about 40 per cent down on what we need. Anyone got any ideas for a new plan of action tomorrow?' Of all the animals with which we share this planet, we are the only ones able to jointly reflect on what has happened, and plan our future ventures accordingly.

Charles Darwin's theory of evolution is often summed up as 'the survival of the fittest', but this does not just mean that the most capable individuals win out under difficult conditions. It means that those best adapted to their environment are more likely to survive and reproduce. Over time, if they pass on their inherited advantages to the next generation, their offspring will become more numerous than the descendants of those that are less 'fit'. So, we need to consider the *communities* that proved the best at surviving. In the development of our species, a key advantage that emerged was the capacity of a group of humans to put their heads together and consider their collective circumstances. This became possible, for the first time in the history of the world, through the emergence of language.

Our language differs from the communication systems of other creatures in that it is not simply a medium for transmitting and receiving information. In fact, transmitting information accurately through spoken language can be quite problematic. The cognitive psychologist Steven Pinker once wrote: 'Simply by making noises with our mouths we can reliably cause precise new ideas to arise in each other's minds.'[1] If only that were the case! If it were so, a primary school teacher who gave a class a specific set of instructions could expect to find every child then doing exactly the same thing, which every teacher knows never happens.

About a decade ago, I heard Pinker give what I thought was a clear and interesting presentation in Cambridge. Discussing it afterwards with others in attendance, it soon became obvious that we each had rather different views on exactly what points he had made. Our interpretations of what we had heard – the same collection of sounds – were not the same. This is not meant as a criticism of Pinker's presentation, because it stimulated a lively discussion. In fact, after that conversation, we each came away with a better understanding of the content of his lecture, and had changed our minds about some aspects we may have misunderstood. Talk can be an unreliable medium for transmitting precise information, but it can be wonderful for sparking people to think creatively and constructively together.

Language enables us to do more than interact: we can use it to think collectively – to *interthink*.* Language

* Lyn Dawes and I invented the term 'interthinking', and, true to its meaning, neither of us is sure who first proposed it. It is explained in more detail in Littleton, K. & Mercer, N. (2013). *Interthinking: Putting talk to work*. Abingdon: Routledge.

enables members of a group to combine their individual mental capabilities to address issues of shared concern. We can use it to describe to others what we see and know – to 'model' the world, to share perceptions (or preconceptions) and jointly consider trajectories beyond our immediate circumstances. We can learn from past mistakes. We can imagine alternative futures. Language has also enabled us to transcend the limitation faced by other animals of having to adapt to the environment in which they find themselves. Instead, we can act together to change the world around us to suit the needs of our community.

In the 1990s, the evolutionary psychologist Robin Dunbar introduced the concept of the 'social brain', and in doing so became one of the first to propose that human intelligence is intrinsically social: we operate effectively in complex social networks.[2] One of our special capabilities is that we can infer the mental states and intentions of other people. For example, neuroscientists have revealed that we respond to subtle social signals as we interact, even if we are not always consciously aware of doing so. From these signals, we try to make sense of what others are thinking – and perhaps predict what they are likely to do. But, unlike our primate relatives, we have another means for gaining relevant information: we can listen to what they say. On the basis of what we see and hear, we can try to consider the world from their point of view. This is known as constructing a 'theory of mind'. It seems no other creatures have this ability to imagine another individual's perspective, except in a very rudimentary form. Most of us take this ability for granted – but its importance is highlighted by the difficulties that some people, such as those who are autistic, have in navigating social encounters.[3]

Evolutionary psychologists like Dunbar were trying to understand how individuals evolved to cope with the informational and emotional complexity of communal life. They were focused on how, in their everyday lives, individual humans became able to use the information they garnered from socialising to handle conflict, and to manipulate others to serve their own ends. Their model of social intelligence, then, was still essentially individualistic – ironically, I think it helped to perpetuate the error of understanding 'survival of the fittest' as an individual issue. We need a different model, based on the emergence of our capacity to interthink. This will help us see more clearly how language relates to our social kind of intelligence, which enables us to engage socially and cognitively with each other in order to pursue common goals and ensure the success of our species.

Human intelligence is 'social' because we are able to think together in order to get things done. Being able to 'theorise' someone's intentions does not just allow me to take social control of an encounter. I can't deny that I might do so, but far more often I have a different objective. I talk with another person to discover what we have in common, and how we can accrue more knowledge together. Our pooled knowledge provides the basis for developing a joint strategy. Talking enables us to build up that common knowledge by incorporating new ideas that each individual brings to our meeting. It can also reveal differences in what we each believe and value, and such differences may fuel a debate or argument. As long as things do not become fractious, talk can generate a dialogic process that spirals onwards, hopefully towards a new shared understanding.

The connection to education should, I hope, be crystalising. Through becoming sensitive to the limits of someone's understanding, we can assess what they know and what they don't. If we find out what they lack, we are able to help them learn. In evolutionary terms, the emergence of this communicative process of education was vital. It enabled a human community to share the useful knowledge gained by each generation, so that their offspring did not need to start again from scratch. Moreover, members of a community could question received wisdom, and so improve the shared body of knowledge through dialogue. Language evolved as the toolkit for education. It allows us to jointly engage in the iterative processes of sharing, planning, acting, reacting, evaluating and revising. Education systems are specially designed cultural artefacts for doing just that.

As humans, then, we are able to use language to link our brains together to create a sort of mega-brain. The neuroscientist Hannah Critchlow, in her book *Joined-up Thinking*, suggests that we should think of intelligence as embodied in collaborative activity, rather than in terms of individuals' test scores.[4] She shares my view that humanity's success has been enabled by groups 'chipping away at problems for years, decades, if necessary'. We need to keep promoting collective thinking, especially at a time when our species faces serious challenges to its survival, from climate change to pandemics, that cannot be overcome by individual action. But I think we also need to recognise how important language abilities – oracy skills – are for this kind of productive collaboration.

Let's go back again to our evolutionary past. A very long time ago, our primate ancestors took an enormous risk: they ditched the certainty of instinct for the promise of learning. I do not mean, of course, that some hominids sat down in a cave and made a gamble together. But in some more amorphous, biological way, that change took place. Most animals, from ants to albatrosses to antelopes, have instinctive behavioural strategies hard-wired into their brains. That means when they are born, the young of many species know what they need to do. They start life primed to survive. This works, as long as the environment that has shaped the evolution of their instincts does not alter too much. They have evolved to fit a particular ecological niche: a match has been made between the inherited characteristics of the species and their environmental conditions. As I write, the swifts have recently departed from my home town: I miss their cries and aerobatics, but I knew they would leave. A new generation of birds did not need to be persuaded to fly south to Africa, away from the English winter. It is instinctive: they were born with the imperative to migrate.

The bees' waggle dance is also instinctive: young worker bees do not have to learn it from a previous generation. But it has only evolved to suit one fixed purpose – communicating about the location of food sources. If, instead of inheriting a fixed, ready-made communication system, a species opts for one that has to be learned through experience and which can be modified, that species becomes more able to adapt collectively to suit environmental shifts. Human language represents such a system. Novel experiences or concepts may need new words to describe them, but those words can be invented – such as permacrisis, adultification, podcast or interthinking. The evolution of language enabled our ancestors to become the first creatures able to describe and define new challenges, and to plan how to deal with them together. Perhaps our heightened ability to interthink was an advantage we had over our Neanderthal cousins.

Our ancestors sacrificed the elegant reliability of a hard-wired communication system for one that we have to learn to use, but which enables more flexibility and creativity. As young humans, we inherit the distinctive capability for acquiring a language – one that is organised into words, tenses and sentences. The catch is, though, that to become language users, youngsters need a lot of relevant experience, and a lot of help. They do not just need to acquire the knowledge of language – they have to have to learn to use it *well*. To become capable speakers and listeners, they need to be involved in its joint use, in dialogue with others. Children don't learn words from dictionaries, they take them from other people's mouths.[5]

There is another very profound and important way that language is bound up with children's development, and with our very nature as human beings. Through language, children do not only develop as communicators, they develop as thinkers. From an educational perspective, oracy is not just about developing communication skills, it is about developing thinking skills. We know how to help young people become better communicators: and we know that that their academic achievement can be promoted through productive dialogue. I will say more about this, and the role of parents and other carers in children's cognitive development, in the next chapter. If we want the members of each new generation to succeed in their personal and collective endeavours, we need to provide them with an educational experience which will help them make the most of their unique evolutionary heritage.

2. An Early Start to Oracy

Babies learn the sounds of language, and start to use them, well before they can produce words or understand what they hear. In 2024, a video went viral on TikTok of a nineteenth-month-old toddler in Liverpool called Orla chatting with her mother, in which Orla's contributions were not words, but 'babbles'.[1] Two things were striking about this clip. The first was that Orla was clearly having a kind of conversation with her mother, in which they each took turns, even though she used no real words. The second was that she was 'talking' in an obvious Scouse accent, reflecting her mother's way of speaking. The video provided a great example of the language behaviour of a young child, and of how a parent can engage with them – but what Orla did was not unusual. From a very early age, children can take part in the to-and-fro of conversation: they can engage in dialogue. And by the age of 9–10 months, most babies' babbling already sounds like the language they hear around them.

Orla's mother was doing the right things to get her started as a speaker and listener. She treated her daughter as someone who had something to say. Simply spending time talking with young children is one of the most useful ways an adult can contribute to their linguistic and cognitive development. As the poet and former Children's Laureate Michael Rosen puts it:

> One of the best things we can do with young children is to have interesting and enjoyable conversations with them. What this means is that as we go about our activities whether at home or at nursery, playgroups, playgrounds, the child-minding situation, or out and about, we should make a special effort to answer children's questions, point out things that interest us, involve children in helping and planning what to do next, whether that's putting out things to play, tidying up, where to visit or whatever.[2]

'Contingent talk'[3] is when an adult picks up a topic in which a child is already showing an interest, and builds the conversation on that foundation. Doing that has been found to be far more effective for encouraging a child's active participation than if an adult tries to introduce a topic of their own. Opportunities to generate contingent talk are likely to arise when a child and an adult are already jointly involved in an activity – solving a problem, making something together or talking about a book they are reading. Of course, good conversations do not necessarily run on prepared scripts. Some of the best support for children's oracy development will probably come from using language with them simply to have fun. But there are some key strategies that can help to get children talking and thinking:

1. If the child asks questions, provide clear and relevant answers.
2. If the child asks 'Why . . . ?', give a reason. In this way you offer a model to the child of how to reason and use key words such as 'because' and 'if'.
3. Ask the child some 'open' questions (which don't require 'right answers') to find out what they think about a topic, and don't take over if they need time to think.
4. Follow up what the child has said, asking them to think again, explain or elaborate their ideas, and so stimulate further thought.
5. Instead of simply telling the child how to do something, encourage them to think what they already know that might enable them to do it.
6. Encourage the child to recall events from the past, by providing prompts and support, perhaps to create a story.
7. Use 'What if . . .' and other openers to ask the child to imagine, predict or design their own response.

8. During activities, think aloud with children about what is going on: 'This is going well. But I wonder what might happen if we add another brick to the tower.'
9. As conversation proceeds, listen and respond to the child, bringing in relevant information and ideas, and ask the child what they want to add. [4]

To make things less abstract, here are some examples of how talk between an adult carer and a child might proceed. They have been adapted from actual, recorded conversations to illustrate how an interaction can go one way, or another. In the first, Maddy, aged three and a half, and her mother are in the living room. Her mother is sorting some clothes, putting some into a bag for the charity shop and others into a pile to throw away. There are many ways that the conversation could go: each could have a different impact on the child. Here are two possible ways:

Version 1

Maddy: Why are those going in there? (*Pointing to the discard pile.*)
Mum: Because they're no good, they're falling apart.
Maddy: But wouldn't they be good for summer?
Mum: For summer! No, like I said, they're falling apart.
Maddy: OK. (*Both fall silent*)

Version 2

Maddy: Why are those going in there? (*Pointing to the discard pile.*)
Mum: Because they're no good, they're falling apart.
Maddy: But wouldn't they be good for summer?
Mum: For summer! Whatever do you mean? Why would they be good for summer?
Maddy: Because they let the wind in, through the holes.
Mum: Oh, I see, you mean if we were hot?
Maddy: Yes. You said, 'I wish there was more wind.'
Mum: Do you remember where we were when I said that?
Maddy: (*Pause*) No. Where were we?
Mum: On a bus going to town.

In the first version, Maddy's mother gives a sensible reason for her actions. She is surprised by Maddy's remark about the clothes being 'good for summer' – but she doesn't find out what lies behind it. She seems to have no interest in what Maddy is thinking. Instead, she just repeats herself. This effectively ends the train of thought. In the second, when Maddy's mother is surprised by Maddy's remark, she asks Maddy to explain what she means. Maddy goes further, though she doesn't make herself entirely clear. Her mother asks her another question. This prompts Maddy to share more of her thoughts, which leads on to discussion about a past event. Children who talk about an experience remember it more clearly than an experience they have not talked about.[5] We can see that the second scenario encourages the child not only to *give a reason*, but to practise using language to *explain* and *recall.*

In another example, Evan, aged four, and his father are putting together a model spaceship from a kit:

Version 1

Evan: (*Holding a red piece of plastic.*) This won't fit on.
Dad: Wait a minute, I'm fixing this bit.
Evan: It won't fit.
Dad: OK, give it to me. (*Takes the piece and eventually fits it on to a spaceman's belt.*) There we are.
Evan: Is it done now?
Dad: Nearly.

Version 2

Evan: (*Holding a red piece of plastic.*) This won't fit on.
Dad: Wait a minute, I'm fixing this bit.
Evan: It won't fit
Dad: OK, let's have look. What do you think this piece is for?
Evan: For a gun – the handle.
Dad: Why do you think that?

Evan: 'Cos it's red

Father: 'Cos it's red – red like what?

Evan: Like the guns on the box. (*Points to the picture on the packaging of the kit.*)

Dad: Oh, I see. Well perhaps you're right; perhaps it goes with the spaceman. Where have you been trying to fit it?

Evan: Here. (*Points to spaceman's belt.*)

Dad: Ah. Why not try it the other way up?

Evan: OK. Yes!

In the first scenario, the toy is completed efficiently, but Evan has little opportunity for learning, either about assembly or about linguistic problem-solving. In the second, his father isn't so eager to take over the job – and asks some questions. He finds out what Evan thinks, asks him for a reason for his opinion, and uses talk to enable his son to see where the piece fits. In this way, Evan gets the chance to develop his skills in *explaining* and *justifying his ideas*. He also gains the confidence to complete the toy without help.

It is crucial that we encourage young children to play and explore independently, without too much adult intervention. But children can't discover everything about the world for themselves – and why should they have to, when so much is known already? They are often very glad to have things explained to them, if the time is right. The Estonian researcher Pirko Tõugu and her colleagues captured some parents having conversations with young children aged four to make shared sense of the Covid pandemic.[6] Here is their example of a German parent and child doing this:

Child: Eh, I know what we are not allowed to do. Namely, we are not allowed to cuddle with each other.
Parent: Mhm. With nobody?
Child: But only with our families.
Parent: Mhm. And do you know why?
Child: Because otherwise, because we don't know whether they have Corona.
Parent: Hm, do you know why you stayed home for so long?
Child: Because of the virus.
Parent: Because of the virus, exactly. Do you remember what's going on with the virus?
Child: All people sick.
Parent: Exactly. A lot of people got sick. And because of that?
Child: Because of that?
Parent: You weren't allowed to go to the kindergarten, right?
Child: Right.
Parent: And what else happened? Who wasn't allowed to go to work in the beginning?
Child: Mom.

This kind of interaction not only helps children to develop their oracy skills, but also helps them learn to use talk to think with another person – to interthink.

Any parent knows that conversations with children can sometimes be difficult. A child may be tired, hungry and out of sorts, and not always eager to learn. And most of us are not gifted with unlimited patience. We cannot always be having careful, thoughtful negotiations with children. Some things need no discussion; 'Stop at the side of the road!', 'Don't touch the iron!', 'No, you can't take your seat belt off!' But even inflexible rules may make more sense to a child if they are backed up with reasons – though of course this can only happen in a situation when there is time to do so.

As well as speaking to children, we also need to use our listening skills. We need to pay attention to what they say. We may get fascinating glimpses into a child's perspective. This can help us to appreciate what they do, or do not, understand. Conversations with others can inform children's everyday observations and correct their misconceptions. For example, here is an exchange between Rilla, aged four, and her childminder Natalie who were at the river feeding ducks:

Natalie: Lots of ducks. What do you think they are covered in, Rilla?

Rilla: Silk.

Natalie: Silk – hmm – not feathers? How do you think they float?

Rilla: They swim (*watches the ducks*), but in the water you can only see their back legs.

Natalie: Back legs? How many legs do they have?

Rilla: Four.

Natalie: Well! Only two, really. They've turned their front legs into wings, I think.

Rilla: (*In amused disbelief*) Hah!

After this conversation, Natalie found some picture books about birds in the library, and she and Rilla spent some time looking at them and drawing different birds.

Children may also notice the ways words are related by sound, although this can cause some initial confusion. For example, Charlie, aged four, was walking by the river with his uncle Bobby when this interaction took place:

Bobby: Can you see the baby swans, Charlie?

Charlie: They're not called baby swans, they're called (*thinking hard*) magnets.

Bobby: Ha! You nearly got it right. They're called cygnets – cygnets.

Charlie: Cygnets.

Here you can see Charlie trying to recall and use a new word he has learned. Noticing the ways some words sound similar, children can become fascinated with jokes, which often involve wordplay. They learn that there is a pattern to some jokes: you ask someone a question, the person replies and then you tell them the 'punchline'. But it usually takes children a while to understand quite what makes them funny. In this next extract, Paula, a parent, and Meg, aged four, listen while Gareth, aged six, tells a joke:

Gareth: How do you get an astronaut's baby to sleep?
Paula: Oh. We don't know. How do you get an astronaut's baby to sleep?
Gareth: You rock it! See. Rocket.

(*Paula and Meg laugh. Later Meg approaches Paula.*)

Meg: How does a baby cow get to sleep?
Paula: I don't know. How?
Meg: In a rocket.
Paula: Oh. Haha.
Meg: Do you get the joke?
Paula: Mm, I'm not sure.
Meg: Because cows don't usually go in spaceships.

Meg clearly needs to refine her joke-telling abilities – but she has already learned how to construct one. On the other hand, in this example, Kelly, aged three, has already learned how to make a joke that depends on a subtle understanding of different ways the verb 'to love' can be used:

Kelly: Mummy, do you love me?
Mother: Yes, of course.
Kelly: Do you love me to *hit* you? Ha, ha!

Songs, rhymes and poems offer accessible and enjoyable wordplay. Discovering the rhythms of language, through lyrics and poems, helps develop children's understanding of the structure of words. For example, a simple nursery rhyme such as 'Jack and Jill' helps children to appreciate the way some words are made up of more than one syllable: 'Jack and Jill went up the hill to fetch a pail of wa-ter'. And if children are encouraged to follow the words on a page as they sing, they will begin to see that similar-sounding words also look similar (Jill/hill, wa-ter/af-ter). This kind of activity can therefore help develop both oracy and literacy skills.

The Ancient Greek scribe Herodotus tells us that in around 600 BCE the Egyptian pharaoh Psammetichus (also known as Psamtik) kept two children isolated from any human contact to see whether, without any input, they would naturally speak Phrygian or Egyptian.[7] It was reported that, on being released, one child said the word '*becos*', the Phrygian word for bread. We now know, of course, that they would know neither language: though, being inventive beings, the children would probably devise some way of communicating with each other. Without being immersed in language, children cannot acquire it; the richness of their language environment will shape their speaking and listening development.

Since the early twentieth century, there have been concerns around the globe about whether all children in a society have a sufficiently stimulating early language experience.[8] Ideas about quite what this should involve have mainly focused on the ways in which, and the extent to which, parents talk with their children. In 1992, Betty Hart and Todd Risley published their research based on one-hour recordings made in the homes of forty-two families in the American Midwest, recorded over a period of two and half years. They chose some families who were wealthy, some of middle income and some with low incomes, including some dependent on welfare payments.[9] They reported that children from the poorest families heard significantly fewer words than those in the wealthiest households. Hart and Risley described this as a '30-million-word gap'. They claimed that this helped to explain different levels of academic attainment by children from different social backgrounds. As well as looking at the number of words children heard at home, Hart and Risley also assessed the *quality* of the talk. This included the ways in which adults responded to children. For example, how often did they ask them questions, encourage or reprimand them? They claimed that wealthier parents involved their children in more varied kinds of interactions, thereby providing a more fulfilling talk environment. They suggested that this meant that, in general terms, wealthier children were better prepared for school. Such inequalities might be passed down from one generation to the next. The clear implication was that, if all children were to start school on an equal footing, adults needed to interact more, and in different ways, with the children in their care.

If Hart and Risley's findings were valid, and if the same applied to children in other countries, it would certainly be a cause for concern. However, not everyone within the research community has accepted their findings, or the conclusions they drew.[10] Some criticise the design and scale of their study: forty-two families are not many, and recordings were made while researchers were present, which might inhibit some family conversations. Another criticism is that the assessments of the quality of language were biased to favour middle-class expression. That is, middle-class parents might not speak with their children in ways that are intrinsically 'better' for children's linguistic and cognitive development, but the way they use their words is similar to a teacher.[11] For example, Hart and Risley found that wealthier parents asked their children more questions. Becoming familiar with question-and-answer exchanges may well be useful preparation for school; but rather than being a key feature for development, might this simply reflect the ways schools embody the culture and language habits of the middle class? If this were the case, it is school culture that needs to change, rather than some parents' conversational styles.

This kind of debate can quickly descend into pointless hair-splitting about who is more to blame for some children's lack of educational success – parents or teachers. However, there is little doubt that the early language experience of children does vary considerably. In 2019, Douglas Sperry, Linda Sperry and Peggy Miller reported their research in the USA, which involved many more families than Hart and Risley's, and they made more careful and more extensive recordings.[12] They still found significant variation in the number of words children heard at home, though the differences between families within the same communities were so great that no clear links with relative wealth could be made. The amount and kinds of talk British children are involved with at home has been found to vary considerably, too.[13]

We also have some interesting, if worrying, reports about the language experience of young children during the Covid pandemic. When the British lockdown began in 2021, my Oracy Cambridge colleagues and I were working with around eighty early years teachers on an oracy project in Birmingham. Their schools were closed for extended periods. As they welcomed their students back, the teachers told us that they were struck by the dramatic range of spoken language capabilities within any one class, compared with pre-pandemic times. It was not just the extent of different children's vocabulary, but their comprehension of what was said, and their willingness to speak and listen. For some children, it seemed lockdown had provided more opportunities than usual for interaction with parents who were working from home, who could engage in play and even do some home-schooling. For others, lockdown seemed to have been a period of social isolation, with few opportunities for dialogue. This left those children less well equipped to engage in the teaching-and-learning talk of the classroom.

Our Birmingham teachers were not alone in their experience. In 2024, a survey found that more than half of 500 British teachers reported that an increasing number of children were falling behind in their vocabulary development, compared with previous years. Ninety-five per cent of those teachers believed that school closures and disruptions during the pandemic contributed to a 'widening vocabulary gap'.[14] Internationally, a project led by the University of Oslo assessed the vocabularies of 1,742 children aged 8–36 months across thirteen countries and in twelve languages, at the beginning and end of the first lockdown period in 2020.[15] Their most striking finding was that children who spent less time sitting passively in front of a screen, and whose caregivers read more to them, showed the largest vocabulary gains. In fact, this was a far better predictor of children's development than their parents' educational background.

Language development is not just a matter of acquiring vocabulary. However, if you have more words at your disposal, then you have better resources for making sense of the world and expressing yourself. An enriched vocabulary is not only important for children's development as speakers and listeners: children learn the meanings of words through talking, which can help them to read and write. As the educational researcher James Britton once put it, 'Writing and reading float on a sea of talk.'[16]

So what can we learn from all this research on early language experience? I think more light and less heat might be generated by shifting the focus away from comparisons between the language habits of richer and poorer families, and focusing more on what kinds of early language experiences are most likely to help all children develop. It is surely uncontroversial to say that all children need to be encouraged and enabled to express their thoughts clearly, to have the world explained to them, to listen attentively, to ask questions about things they do not understand, to provide reasons for their opinions and reflect on experiences they share with other people. Those are not middle-class ways of using language; they are ways of using language that promote the development of knowledge and understanding.

Some children, perhaps because of their home experience, will need more encouragement than others to engage in talk. To suggest that, in order to avoid social bias, teachers should not encourage reluctant children to communicate in these ways is seriously misguided. To treat every child joining a class as being equally capable at speaking and listening would amount to ignoring individual differences. A 'one size fits all' approach to education cannot possibly be justified.

The reality is that a primary school class of twenty-six students – the average number in British schools in 2023 – will include children who have reached very different stages of language development. That makes any teacher's job difficult: smaller classes would of course make life better for everyone involved. But if there is to be equality of educational opportunity, every teacher must be a teacher of oracy – and that will involve taking account of each child's developmental level. This is already expected for literacy and numeracy.

Some useful resources have been developed to help children who need extra support to develop their language skills. A good example is the Nuffield Early Language Intervention (NELI), developed at the universities of Oxford, Sheffield and York. Targeted at 4–5-year-olds, it offers a combination of an assessment scheme, some professional development training for teachers and a twenty-week programme of activities.[17] An independent evaluation of NELI found that children who participated in the programme made, on average, four months more progress in their language skills than children in the same schools who were not involved.[18]

One of the first people to link language use to children's development was the Russian Lev Vygotsky.[19] He died at the early age of thirty-seven in 1933, though he achieved a great deal in his short life. He seems to have been a remarkable man, prominent in Moscow literary circles in the 1920s, who directed plays and wrote on a wide range of subjects, including art and Marxist theory. His main work, though, was as a psychologist who specialised in the education of children with learning difficulties. His work was innovative, but it was suppressed by the Stalinist regime, which preferred the simpler, stimulus-response psychology of Ivan Pavlov and his dogs. Vygotsky's ideas only became known years later through the efforts of Western psychologists like Jerome Bruner and Michael Cole.[20]

Working with young children led Vygotsky to redefine the relationship between language development and cognitive development – and in quite a radical way. He suggested that once a child acquires language, their thinking is transformed forever. Imagine, for example, a child first witnessing, and then becoming involved in, a reasoned discussion: a conversation in which participants offer their points of view, support them with evidence and then try to draw some agreed conclusions. Experiencing such discussions enables children not only to learn how to use language to interthink but also teaches them how to carry on a kind of reasoned dialogue within their individual minds – on the one hand this, on the other hand that – and carry it through to a rational conclusion. Being able to do so is part of becoming an 'educated' person. Without the experience of reasoning with others, children would not have a model of reasoning that would allow them to construct their own internal rationality. This is why the quality of young children's language experience at home, and later in school, is crucial for their personal development and educational progress. In Chapters 6 and 7, I will describe some practical ways that teachers can help develop ways of talking and thinking in the classroom, which build on Vygotsky's work.

For some children, whatever their home experience, the development of spoken communication skills is not a straightforward process. They may have hearing, speaking or learning difficulties, so a full understanding of oracy development needs to take account of any child's additional needs, which may include neurodiversity.

Autistic children often find it difficult to understand subtle social rules, or to cope in a situation when several people are speaking. They may be helped by having the importance of some conversational behaviours explained – such as saying 'yes', nodding to indicate comprehension or taking conversational turns.[21] Equally important, though, is that others appreciate these communication difficulties. For example, developmental language disorder is a term now used to describe problems with speaking and understanding spoken language which cannot be attributed to any specific cause.[22] An articulate sufferer from this condition, Lily Farrington, has explained what it felt like to be a school student whose difficulties were not recognised until she was fifteen years old: 'When people talk . . . it feels like you have to catch the words as they are falling, but you can't catch them all and you're missing out on what's been said.'[23] In 2024, the charity Speech and Language UK estimated that 1.9 million children in the UK have some kind of 'speech, language, communication needs'.[24] In this book, I cannot provide comprehensive advice for young people with special educational needs, or for their parents and carers, but such support is widely available.[25]

I have so far referred to 'language' in general. But at least half the people in the world speak more than one language. Sometimes parents have asked me: is it good to encourage a young child to become bilingual? Until the middle of the twentieth century, it was commonly claimed that growing up as bilingual could cause problems by 'overloading' children's mental capacities. However, according to the research evidence available today, learning to speak more than one language offers significant cognitive benefits. For example, bilingual children are better than monolinguals at ignoring distractions when engaged in a task.[26] It may be that having learned to make linguistic choices has enhanced their ability to focus. This may also be why the acquisition of multiple languages has a positive effect on children's 'executive functioning' – the ability to set and pursue goals. Bilinguals also perform better in tasks requiring lateral thinking and creativity.[27] It is as though they have acquired not just one, but two toolkits for modelling the world, each of which can offer a different reality. This is why the translation of works of literature, for example, requires great expertise. Bilingual adults are better at creative tasks, too, especially if they have public speaking experience in the second language. In addition to these cognitive benefits, there is of course the joy of becoming an active member of more than one language community, with access to diverse cultural resources.[28]

Until about the age of twelve, most children find it amazingly easy to learn more than one language. (In later years, in my experience, it becomes much harder!) I still meet bilingual parents who say they are only speaking the language of school, such as English, with their children at home, because they think to do otherwise might hinder their child's educational progress. I try to convince them that their fears are groundless. If family members normally speak a different language than the one used in school, they should not feel it necessary to switch for the sake of children's educational and social development. They would be better advised to sustain their heritage language at home, as children will readily pick up the spoken language of mainstream society beyond their front door. It is also worth noting that most oracy skills – like those involved in making public speeches and working well in a team – are not especially language specific. I was recently asked to judge an international English public-speaking competition: the winner was a French sixteen-year-old whose mother told me he was also fluent in Mandarin.

Oracy development begins in the earliest years of life; and it is essentially a social activity. As novice pilots, we do not learn by flying solo. We need the active support of people around us to make progress. The conversational life of the home should play a vital part, but there also needs to be an adequate provision of nursery education, with suitably trained teachers; and children with special language needs may require support throughout their school lives. Young children need guidance in becoming effective speakers and listeners. Providing that guidance requires patience, time and respect from adults, which are also qualities a young child can develop through engaging in thoughtful conversations.

3. The Oracy Skills Framework

Literacy skills have long been in the limelight. Many detailed specifications for how children should be taught to read, and how their skills should be assessed, have been developed and refined. In 1956, the International Reading Association, since renamed the International Literacy Association, was established. Its conferences are large; its journals for researchers and teachers well funded. There is nothing equivalent, yet, for oracy.

Oracy skills can be taught, just as the skills of literacy and numeracy already are, everywhere. But my Cambridge colleagues and I could find nothing that set out the skills for communicating effectively through talk in a systematic, useful way. So in 2012, working with School 21, we consulted many professionals – linguists, speech therapists, English teachers, language teachers, drama teachers, speech trainers, educational consultants and experts in assessment – to create the Oracy Skills Framework:*

* A glossary of terms is available online: https://oracycambridge.org/wp-content/uploads/2020/06/The-Oracy-Skills-Framework-and-Glossary.pdf

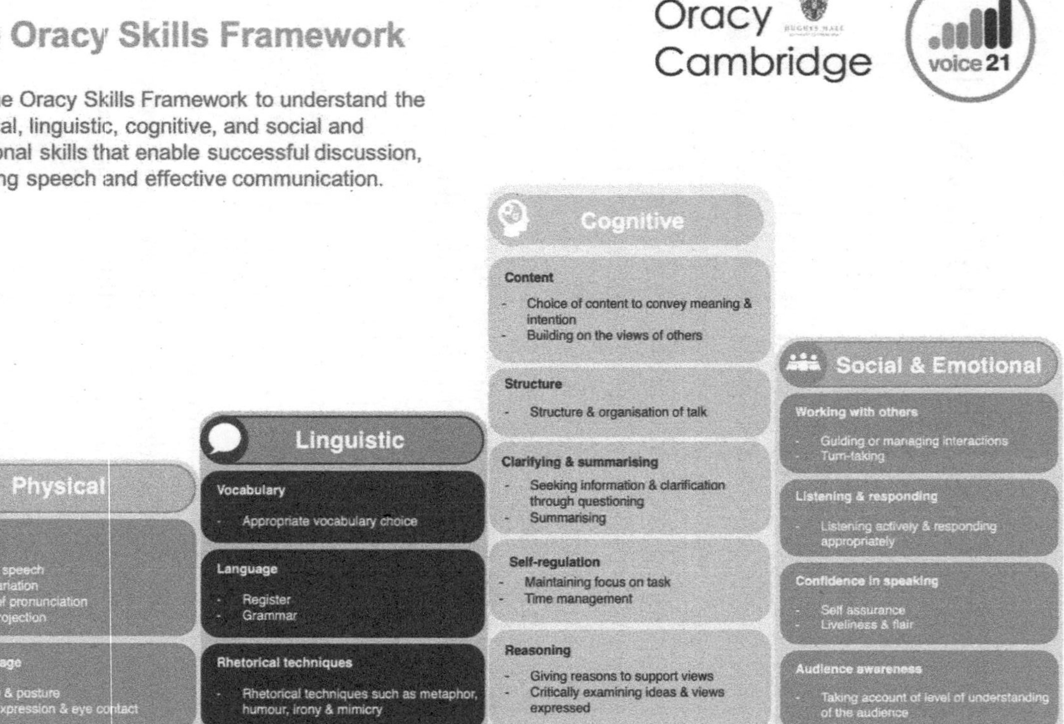
The Oracy Skills Framework
Oracy Cambridge
voice 21
Use the Oracy Skills Framework to understand the physical, linguistic, cognitive, and social and emotional skills that enable successful discussion, inspiring speech and effective communication.
Physical
Voice
- Pace of speech
- Tonal variation
- Clarity of pronunciation
- Voice projection
Body language
- Gesture & posture
- Facial expression & eye contact
Linguistic
Vocabulary
- Appropriate vocabulary choice
Language
- Register
- Grammar
Rhetorical techniques
- Rhetorical techniques such as metaphor, humour, irony & mimicry
Cognitive
Content
- Choice of content to convey meaning & intention
- Building on the views of others
Structure
- Structure & organisation of talk
Clarifying & summarising
- Seeking information & clarification through questioning
- Summarising
Self-regulation
- Maintaining focus on task
- Time management
Reasoning
- Giving reasons to support views
- Critically examining ideas & views expressed
Social & Emotional
Working with others
- Guiding or managing interactions
- Turn-taking
Listening & responding
- Listening actively & responding appropriately
Confidence in speaking
- Self assurance
- Liveliness & flair
Audience awareness
- Taking account of level of understanding of the audience

The Oracy Skills Framework helps teachers to identify the oracy strengths and weaknesses of students, and to create personal oracy profiles. Some students might be adept at projecting their voice in a public event, but are not good at 'listening attentively and responding appropriately' when put into a small group. Others might not pronounce or project their words clearly when speaking in public, but they may be good at 'guiding and managing interactions', and working with others to resolve a dilemma, through 'seeking information and clarification'.

In a given social situation, only some of these skills will be involved in making communication effective. In a job interview, say, the normal expectation would be that a speaker should stay on topic, and avoid slang, casual humour and interrupting; they should use a formal register. In a casual chat among friends, however, maintaining a formal style would, to say the least, be odd. This might all seem obvious – but the nature of the differences between appropriate registers may not be obvious to all young people, especially if they have had little experience of formal events. Similarly, 'facial expression and eye contact' are vital when face-to-face, but irrelevant if talking on the phone. 'Voice projection' can be important when making a speech, but 'listening actively and responding appropriately' would not be relevant. However, the opposite would be the case for people working together in a small team.

'Body language', or 'non-verbal communication' (NVC) skills – gesture, posture, eye contact and facial expressions – are included in the framework, as they certainly can affect the meaning and impact of what we say. But I want to counter a familiar misconception about their importance. Elizabeth Stokoe, a leading authority on spoken language and author of *Talk: The science of conversation*,[1] writes that when she is giving lectures, people often challenge her with the 'statistic' that 93 per cent of communication is through body language, with language only performing a minor role. She has to tell them that this is a myth. If it were true, we would not be able to hold perfectly good conversations on the phone or in the dark. And many body language 'signals' only make sense in the context of what is actually said. Stokoe also warns us to beware of some cardinal features of communication training programmes, such as the imperatives that a customer receptionist should begin by asking, 'How are you this morning?'; or a call centre operator should say 'Hello, you are speaking to David today.' In fact, these are such false attributes of a normal interaction between strangers that they can damage rapport, rather than establishing it.

Nevertheless, the 'physical' strand of the Oracy Skills Framework should certainly be given direct attention. For some children, it can be vital to encourage and reassure them that their voices deserve to be heard. And, as with any skilled physical activity, voice production and control can be improved through training (as performances by the best stage actors demonstrate well). The development of physical oracy skills need not be restricted to drama lessons.

When it comes to assessing capabilities in relation to the Oracy Skills Framework, it is easier to do so for some kinds of oracy activities than others. By its nature, speech is transient; and though it can be recorded for closer analysis, that takes expertise and is very time-consuming. I have judged competitions for the English-Speaking Union and the Speakers Trust in which young people make speeches and enact debates before an audience. There, I feel reasonably secure in using the criteria I am given to make and justify my judgement. Even so, a judge's perception of a public performance can be influenced by an audience's reception: the assessments of talk are context dependent. How anyone contributes to a group discussion depends a lot on how other participants contribute, so making an individual assessment can be problematic. And I readily admit that assessing knowledge or skills in educational settings can focus attention exclusively on what will be assessed: the history curriculum becomes reduced to just those topics that will figure in the examination; and learning to read becomes reduced to practising for a phonics test.

Nevertheless, despite the inherent difficulties, I believe we should strive to assess oracy so that anyone developing their spoken language skills is able to know what progress they are making.[2] Teachers also need to know if their methods for teaching oracy are working – and to understand which skills a student needs to focus on. A more controversial but nevertheless important reason is that in an education system, time and effort can best be justified if they produce some measurable outcomes. That is why such attention is given to comparisons of attainment across the globe.[3] And, of course, examination grades can open doors to opportunity.

In the 1980s, the nettle of oracy assessment was grasped firmly by the UK's Assessment of Performance Unit (APU). Its language survey monitored thousands of students aged eleven and fifteen, and included tasks designed to assess their oracy skills. The tasks reflected the kinds of experiences students would come across in or out of school; and most required both the interpretation and production of talk. The main conclusion reached by the APU was that it was feasible to monitor speaking and listening performance on a national scale. They reported their finding that 'almost all 11-year-olds can modify their speaking strategies appropriately in accordance with the demands of different tasks and different audiences'.[4]

Although there were criticisms of the APU methods,

they did demonstrate that it is possible to carry out reasonably robust oracy assessments. In 2008, the Assessment of Pupil Progress (APP) framework was launched as a diagnostic scheme for teachers in the UK, which enabled them to track progress and identify targets. It contained four assessment categories for speaking and listening: talking to others, talking with others, talking within role-play and drama, and talking about talk. Following this, the UK Qualifications and Curriculum Development Agency (QCDA) described four strands of relevant oracy skills: listening and responding; speaking and presenting; group discussion and interaction; drama, role-play and performance.[5] Progression was measured by whether pupils could:

- Judge their own and others' skills in spoken language and listening
- Sustain talk and strive for certain effects in formal situations
- Sustain and develop discussion for particular purposes
- Think through issues and problems
- Appreciate and articulate implied meaning
- Apply their learning to complex and unfamiliar demands

In what many saw as a blow to the fortunes of oracy in England, Ofqual, the examinations regulator, announced in 2013 that the speaking and listening component would no longer count towards the GCSE grade for English. Ofqual justified this by their concerns about the validity and reliability of the assessment.[6] One unfortunate and predictable effect, though, was that spoken language skills were then given much less attention in secondary schools.

Outside the school system, the London Academy of Music and Drama (LAMDA) is one organisation which offers assessments of skills in public speaking and presentation. And the Communication Trust provides a set of 'Speech, language and communication progression tools' that can help teachers to identify pupils of various ages who have specific language needs. The Scottish Survey of Literacy includes an assessment of listening and talking that uses group discussion tasks at ages eight, eleven and thirteen.[7]

Internationally, oracy assessment often takes place under a different name. The OECD Programme for International Student Assessment (PISA) includes a test of collaborative problem-solving, using a computer-based simulation, to rate students' ability to work with two or more people.[8] In the USA, the Common Core Standards for English Language Arts, adopted by most states, is a set of guidelines for teachers and parents which gives guidance on what young people are expected to achieve at the end of each grade.[9] For instance, thirteen-year-olds should able to 'follow rules for collegial discussions and decision-making'.[10] However, none of these schemes includes a framework that identifies the full range of skills involved in meeting the assessment criteria, which is why we created the Oracy Skills Framework.

This framework is the basis for the Cambridge Oracy Assessment Toolkit,[11] which covers three important types of spoken communication: 1) a formal presentational speech; 2) an instructional activity whereby one student helps another to complete a specific task; and 3) a group discussion in which three students are asked to reach joint conclusions about a specific topic. A rating scheme enables teachers to score students. By using the toolkit to make both initial and later assessments, a teacher can judge a student's progress over time. Video examples of children performing the tasks, with the ratings they received, are also available online. Although designed for children aged 11–12, the toolkit can be adapted for children who are slightly younger or older.

For some years, my colleagues and I have worked with a group of sixteen Scottish secondary schools in Aberdeen, Aberdeenshire and Angus.[12] Funded by the Wood Foundation, over eighty teachers have now been involved in training workshops and networks, and in leading, and sustaining, oracy as a whole school initiative. Using the Oracy Skills Framework, the schools focus on: 'Oracy as an overt skill set: direct teaching to enable students to use talk to get things done, and to learn effectively.' This initiative is expressly based on the belief that the ability to present confidently, actively question and share their ideas will be important for young people as they progress through education and into the wider world.

Teaching oracy in school does not mean only giving young people more opportunities to practise speaking and listening. It would not be enough to merely encourage the use of spoken language in all curriculum subjects, though I strongly support that, too. There should also be oracy lessons – just as there are maths lessons, for example – in school timetables.

To my surprise, Robin Alexander, an eminent British educational researcher and effective advocate for teachers and their students becoming expert in 'learning through talk', has not encouraged the direct teaching of speaking and listening skills. He seems to think it is not possible, in school, to separate the development of skills from their application in studying subjects such as science or history. Alexander questions whether 'it is actually possible for the teaching of talk to be only about itself'.[13] This is odd, given that the teaching of mathematics has proceeded for a long time on that basis. Students are not only taught about the subject of mathematics, but also how to carry out mathematical operations; I am suggesting nothing different for oracy.

Skills, of any kind, need to be underpinned by knowledge and practice. But the development of meaningful competencies, say in music or sport, commonly involves the development of specific skills. This is often done separately from their use in actual performance. I think many drama teachers would be surprised to find that their efforts to develop students' voice projection, clarity of pronunciation, gesture, pacing and so on through specific workshops were considered misguided or even impossible.

When they arrive at the school gates, we do not expect children to just catch on to literacy or numeracy. We don't assume that they will magically understand punctuation or multiplication without education. So we shouldn't insist that they should just pick up 'listening skills' and 'speaking skills' as they learn about other things. Yet when he was the UK Secretary of State for Education, Michael Gove remained steadfast that more talk in the classroom inevitably means more 'idle chat'. In 2013, he revealed his ignorance of child development by claiming that 'Children naturally learn to talk; they do not naturally learn to read, or to play the violin, or to carry out long division.'[14] To put it mildly, it was dismaying that someone entrusted with a nation's education policy could be so ill-informed. In contrast, in 2024, the newly appointed Secretary of State for Education, Bridget Phillipson, signalled a step change: she wanted to establish a 'curriculum that ensures children and young people leave compulsory education ready for life and ready for work, building the knowledge, skills and attributes young people need to thrive. This includes embedding digital, oracy and life skills in their learning.'[15]

Gove was aligned with what is usually called 'traditional' education, which as well as foregrounding the 'basics', insists that classroom life should primarily consist of teachers talking and students listening. The former teacher, 'influencer' and 'Behaviour Czar' for schools in England, Tom Bennett, who was appointed by Gove, is one of the foremost advocates of this traditional approach. He posted the following comment on X/Twitter in April 2024 in response to the Labour Party's manifesto promise to put oracy into schools: 'Oracy is of course incontestably valuable. But already this has the hallmarks of a bandwagon that will become a Trojan Horse for "well, at least they're talking". As a profession, as a sector, we need to be able to critically challenge any of the outlandish activities and claims that will be made'. Rather than acknowledging the importance of oracy, it seems he would rather jump to conclusions about how the concept will be misapplied.

In October 2023, the *Sunday Times* columnist Robert Colville wrote approvingly of Michaela Community School in London, which enforces an extremely strict classroom regime.[16] This school had achieved a better 'progress' rating from Ofsted inspectors than the oracy flagship institution, School 21. Of this, and the Labour Party's endorsement of oracy in their election manifesto, he wrote: 'This isn't the first time left-wing dogma about education has run into the brick wall of reality.'

Michaela Community School, where teachers apparently insist on total silence in corridors and do not use group-based activities in class, does indeed achieve strong results. But if one looks deeper into what is offered at the this state-funded 'free school' for students aged 11-18 years, its website states that as part of the Personal, Social and Health Education (PSHE) curriculum, students study 'how to make friends', 'how to listen' and 'how to communicate your feelings'.[17] Students are also encouraged to speak out confidently in class. That sounds like a kind of oracy education to me – and apparently a kind that is quite compatible with 'traditional' teaching.

If parents of the most 'privileged' children choose to send their offspring to Eton College, they may expect to be paying for the most traditional kind of education. But the school's website describes 'the importance of teamwork' in the Eton House Maths Challenge, during which students were organised to work collaboratively in groups.[18] Etonians are taught public-speaking skills, the success of which is demonstrated by their disproportionate representation among politicians. The school also offers online oracy education that is described as follows: 'Our Public Speaking Course will improve your ability to speak in all kinds of contexts, from formal speeches in front of an audience to informal presentations in class. You'll learn how to overcome nerves, engage your audience and deal with difficult questions.' Shouldn't this kind of education be available to all students, and not just online?

The schools I hope parents avoid are those that offer a caricature of a traditional education, with fiercely enforced regimes of silent classrooms and rigid uniform regulations, reminiscent of Mr Gradgrind's school in Dickens's *Hard Times*. A young member of my family has been unfortunate enough to attend one that was recently taken over by an Academy Trust. Students are now told they must only speak in reply to teachers' questions and to do so 'in full sentences' – a good rule for making it harder for them to think aloud. My young relative even provided me with audio evidence, gained surreptitiously, of its regime in practice. I heard students being told that infringement of any of the new rules, which included talking to another student during lessons about anything, even the subject matter, would result in them being sent to 'Reflection' – an hour of solitary confinement in which they just sit and are not allowed even to do schoolwork.

As I will explain in Chapter 7, the provision of oracy education is perfectly compatible with the pursuit of outstanding academic results. In fact, it can help students to achieve them. Recent research from the Education Policy Institute has shown that the range of educational attainment among British sixteen-year-olds has increased since the pandemic and that may be connected to the quality of their language experiences.[19]

Spoken language is an essential part of school life, even in schools with 'strict' regimes. Oracy skills are educationally vital from the first day children arrive. But many children do not come to school well prepared to use talk for learning. Lack of oracy skills and self-confidence can mean that some children feel unable to participate fully in activities, leaving them unmotivated and disaffected. Some have special needs that affect their ability to communicate through talk.

Developing oracy skills can, of course, make a difference to the kind of work young people might find when they leave school, as well as preparing them for difficult social situations. If the worst comes to the worst, as Stephen Coleman, professor of political communication, says, young people may find themselves interacting with police officers, solicitors, courts and even prison staff: 'Their hope of these interactions ending safely for them will often depend upon their capacity to express themselves appropriately, not only verbally, but in terms of tone, body language and capacity to formulate their own interests.'[20] In other words, they would be better prepared for such eventualities if they had the benefit of oracy education.

When he was a teacher, my colleague James Mannion led an oracy intervention in his large comprehensive secondary school in south-east England, which had a high proportion of students from deprived homes. Gaining the full support of the school managers and teachers, James was able to sustain his 'Learning skills' programme for three years, involving all students through Years 7–9. He also carried out a systematic evaluation of the programme, finding that: 'A clear pattern emerged from this study: the explicit and relentless focus on oracy education – the fact that we treated oracy as a curriculum to be learned and mastered – developed their confidence. This then spilled over into other areas of their lives – including, but not limited to, learning in other subjects. (They also often spoke and wrote about how this confidence transformed their relationships with their peers and family members).'[21]

Learning speaking and listening skills is not only vital for those who struggle with mainstream education, it can be valuable for academic highflyers, too. A few years ago, the educational psychologist Clara Perez-Adamson came to me with a proposal to research the ways that first-year undergraduates adapted to academic life at Cambridge. In particular, she was interested in whether British students from fee-paying or state-funded schools found this adaptation more or less difficult, and if this related to how their schools prepared them. Clara had been educated mainly outside the UK, and so she could approach this issue, and the students involved, from a detached perspective. The data consisted of twenty interviews with students at two of the oldest, and most traditional, Cambridge colleges.[22] All the students involved had achieved very high academic grades at school in order to gain entry to the university.

The Cambridge approach to university education involves small group discussions between students and their tutor, which are called 'supervisions'. Students are encouraged to talk about their studies and share any problems arising. Tutors may also encourage students to pursue some topics in more depth. We found that students from prestigious private schools typically had no trouble with what this involves. For example, one student said: 'I think [the school] did quite a lot to prepare me for here . . . So I was given mock interviews by various teachers who knew how to challenge me, how to get me thinking in a sort of Oxbridge fashion.' Others commented that their supervisions were akin to sessions in their sixth form, where speaking out and discussion were encouraged.

In contrast, the students from state schools typically found the transition very challenging. One – the first ever from their school to come to Cambridge – said: 'In supervisions I would be asked something and . . . kind of lock, shut down almost rather than trying to think, "well, actually I do know something" . . . I think I was just scared, I was scared of what he was going to ask me.' That student's sixth-form studies had not included any group discussions: the overwhelming emphasis had been on preparing for written examinations. Some state school students said they had felt out of their depth in their first term, and even considered leaving. But being the kind of resilient, determined young people who had succeeded academically so far, they usually overcame their difficulties. In 2015, research by Cambridge Assessment found that students from state schools are far more likely to get a good degree than private school students with similar A-level results.[23] But why should students coming from state schools have to face this kind of problem? Why should sixth formers who go to private schools be better prepared for university life? At Oracy Cambridge, my colleagues and I have been working with the University's Widening Participation team and teachers to help secondary school students develop their communication skills to redress this imbalance.[24]

Oracy education can also be useful in addressing other social disparities. Early this century, language researcher Robin Lakoff found that, at American universities, women students typically participated less in classes than men.[25] In the 1990s, another researcher, Judith Baxter, found that many girls experience difficulties – relative to boys – when they are required to speak in formal, public or unfamiliar contexts.[26] Clare Wagner, head of Henrietta Barnett, a state secondary school for girls in London, noticed even high-achieving students were reluctant to speak out in class, despite the absence of male students. In her 2023 blog, she commented that: 'while girls are recognised to be good at using collaborative talk in small groups, it is still the public voice that is valorised in the world outside school . . . The issue for educators is how to encourage girls to acquire skills that are culturally coded as "masculine".'[27] The answer, as she and others propose, is to provide oracy education that will enable young women to develop the confidence and skills to overcome male dominance in public life. As she says, 'Just the idea of girls and women in society having "diminished voices" should be enough to make every teacher of girls sit and up engage with this topic.'

If we want all young people to find their voices, schools must do three things: teach oracy skills; offer students plenty of opportunities to use, practise and develop their spoken language abilities; and provide them with the knowledge about spoken language which underpins these skills. As oracy is both a skill set and a subject, it can expressly be taught and embedded within all teaching and learning.

4. Talking Proper

A few years ago, a friend of mine was on a train in the United States and got into conversation with a woman sitting opposite. He said he really liked her accent and asked where she was from. 'Kentucky,' she replied. She then said, 'I can tell from your accent that you aren't American – where are you from?'

'Scotland,' he replied.

'Really?' she said, 'But you speak English so well!'

Studying spoken language has always been, for me, a labour of love. For as long as I can remember, I have been interested in talk – and, my mother would probably say, in talking. I went to primary school in rural Lancashire where, like the rest of my schoolmates, I spoke Lancashire dialect, with a Lancashire accent. I use 'accent' here, and throughout this book, to refer to how words are pronounced, and 'dialect' to mean varieties of one language that differ in vocabulary and grammar.

Then we moved to West Cumbria, the north-western edge of the Lake District, where I attended secondary school – and where local people spoke a very different dialect, with a very different accent. We had only moved a hundred miles north, but South Lancashire and West Cumbria were, and still are, places with distinctive cultures and histories. I discovered that Cumbrian dialect had rather glamorous associations with Viking invaders and early Celtic settlers. We learned about the Cumbrian shepherds' counting system, which is related to Welsh: '*Yan, tan, tethera, methera, pip* . . . ' (Both Cymru and Cumbria come from the same roots.) I heard new words and expressions. In rural Lancashire someone might greet me by saying, 'Ar't all reet, lad?', but in Cumbria it would be: 'Hoos te djoan, marra?' Lancastrian children went 'wom' (home) after school, while Cumbrians went 'yam'. What I called a 'hill' was now a 'fell', and a 'brook' was now a 'beck'. I had learned one variety of English and now, through immersion, I was acquiring another. And in doing so, I was also learning about the English language, and how it sustains the identities of communities.

Oracy has three aspects: learning *through* talk, learning *how to* talk and learning *about* talk. Here, I want to focus on the relationship between two of them: learning spoken language skills (learning *how to* talk) and developing an understanding of language itself (learning *about* talk).

There have been futile debates in educational circles in recent years about whether schools should concentrate on imparting knowledge or on developing skills. Strident voices on social media have argued one way or the other, with more heat than light being generated. I say 'futile' because the purpose of education cannot be reduced to either. The most adept people have the relevant knowledge to underpin their skills; but they also know how to get things done. So it should be with oracy. As the 2024 Oracy Commission put it, schools should develop students' communication skills and provide them with knowledge about patterns of language use, language diversity and the relationship between language and culture.[1] We are more likely to appreciate why we communicate in different ways if we understand how spoken language works, and the nature and social significance of accents and dialects. This includes understanding the kinds of regional and local variation that can exist within a language, and how different varieties are rooted in the histories and customs of particular communities and places.

I think most young people would be interested in language variation, not least because it can explain why they may be told there are 'correct' and 'incorrect' ways of speaking. Yet, at the time of writing, you would struggle to find many schools in Britain where the study of the history, nature and varieties of the English language is part of the curriculum. Fortunately, there are some beacons in the wilderness. For example, some of the schools in Aberdeenshire I have worked with are linked to the Buchan Heritage Society, which was founded to celebrate and uphold the cultural traditions of North-east Scotland. The schools teach children about Scottish English and a local variety, known as Doric. As they say: 'For those pupils who are brought up in Doric speaking homes it will broaden their horizons and give their form of speech an importance it has long been denied; for those who have little contact with the local dialect it will open a door of discovery.'[2]

My Lancashire accent was a source of amusement to my new Cumbrian classmates when I read aloud in class: 'You should be a comedian,' said one. For a while, this made me nervous about public speaking – and I got no help from teachers in overcoming my fears. I once avoided school altogether by pretending I had a sore throat when I was meant to speak in assembly. Although I cannot claim to have greatly suffered from negative attitudes to my accent, as a university student I had to get used to southerners making fun of the way I said 'book' ('oo' as in 'school'). I usually restrained myself from laughing at the way they pronounced 'bath' ('bauth'). Other people have not been so lucky. The Scottish comedian Billy Connolly said that his early experiences of working on TV were 'hellish' because of producers who were resistant to letting him speak normally, claiming his Glasgow accent would not be understood.[3] Chloe Alexandria, of the Black Feminist Collective, has written that when she was at university: 'People would always mock students who would pronounce words like "society" and "water" with a working-class twang so like a lot of my peers in certain spaces, I learnt not to.'[4] UK deputy prime minister Angela Rayner, who represents her hometown in Parliament, has faced considerable abuse online because of her Stockport accent. Rayner's own defiant response on X/Twitter was: 'My accent & way in which I speak has again come under attack from some people, I have the same accent as the people I represent, I won't change.' The sociolinguist Rob Drummond has pointed out that women in public roles are particularly disparaged for the way they speak. If they speak forcefully, they are likely to be described as 'shrill', while male equivalents are never criticised in this way.[5]

Attitudes about the way people speak can have a direct influence on interpersonal relations. In 1916, the Irish dramatist George Bernard Shaw wrote in his preface to *Pygmalion*, a play about accents and dialects, that 'It is impossible for an Englishman to open his mouth without making some other Englishman hate or despise him'. Plus ça change. In 2022, the Sutton Trust, a charity which promotes social mobility, reported that 30 per cent of the British university students they surveyed said that they had been 'mocked, criticised or singled out in educational settings due to their accents'.[6] The trust's founder, Sir Peter Lampl, recalls: 'When I moved from Wakefield to Surrey, my broad Yorkshire accent stood out at my new school and resulted in me being mercilessly picked upon and ridiculed, and I learned to develop a Surrey accent in order to fit in. This is a common experience for those who are geographically or socially mobile.'

Back in the 1970s, researchers at the University of Cardiff carried out experiments in which listeners heard actors use different regional accents to relay the same message. This so-called 'matched guise' technique has some flaws – for example, were the actors performing each accent equally well? – but the results were intriguing. They found that the regional accent an actor adopted when presenting an argument affected the judgements of listeners about the speaker's attractiveness, trustworthiness and credibility.[7] More recently, the Accent Bias in Britain project used genuine speakers of different accents to confirm that positive and negative attitudes to ethnic and regional accents of English still persist among the general population.[8] Some accents, such as Devonshire and Yorkshire, seem to be associated with honesty and trustworthiness, while others such as Liverpool and Birmingham, are not. And some British accents are judged more aesthetically pleasing by British listeners than others: for example, an Edinburgh accent is commonly considered more pleasant than a Manchester accent.

The Accent Bias project's sociolinguists also found

that when British listeners were asked to judge the professional competence of candidates in recorded job interviews, regional accents influenced their verdicts. Interestingly, though, there was less bias among younger people, and negative attitudes to regional accents were most entrenched among upper middle-class people who had grown up in southern England. Listeners aged over seventy judged speakers of Multicultural London English as far less likely to succeed if hired by a law firm than did listeners in their twenties.[9] The fact that those listeners were British is important. Americans asked to listen to the interviews did not make the same judgements. They would, no doubt, have their own attitudes about American accents and regional identities. A friend from Tennessee told me that when she first moved to New York she had to get used to people laughing and saying they 'loved her southern twang'. It is not the sounds of an accent that people respond to, but what the accent is taken to represent. For example, stereotypes of Liverpool, Glasgow, Devon or Yorkshire – or of ethnic groups – may be invoked even when listeners cannot see speakers or haven't actually met them.[10]

To be clear: everyone who speaks has an accent. You cannot lose your accent; you can only change it. In the UK, the accent that is typically accorded the highest status is received pronunciation (RP), which historically has been associated with the upper classes and BBC presenters. That does not necessarily mean all reactions to RP will be positive – speakers may be judged as 'posh' or 'snooty'. It all depends on a listener's perspective.

The status of RP is sometimes justified by claiming it is the most accurate representation of how English words should sound. If that is supposed to mean that it most accurately represents in speech the spelling of words, that is unequivocally not true. RP is no more closely related to the ways English words are spelled than, say, the accents of Glasgow, Liverpool or Birmingham. English spelling is notoriously inconsistent compared with languages such as Spanish and Finnish, partly because modern English has its roots in several languages: especially Latin, French, Germanic and Celtic. As any English language learner will have discovered, spelling is no guide to pronunciation. Village names near my home provide a striking example: within ten miles of each other are Broughton (pronounced 'Braw-ton'), Woughton (pronounced 'Wuff-ton') and Loughton (pronounced 'Lou-ton').

Nevertheless, the ways English words are pronounced can be contentious. I have heard British people (usually of my, older, generation) complain about the way many other British speakers pronounce words like 'kettle'. The target of their complaints is what is technically called the 'glottal stop'. The speaker pronounces the 't' in 'kettle' in a way that might be represented in print as 'ke'lle' or 'keh-ul', by rapidly opening and closing the folds of their vocal cords, which comprise the 'glottis'. The glottal stop is a language feature found in several parts of Britain. A more conventional 't' sound, called an 'aspirated "t"', is produced by using the tongue and teeth (and is the first sound in those two words). In American English the glottal stop can be heard in the pronunciation of 'Manhattan' as 'Manha'n'. In Australian English, on the other hand, it does not seem to occur at all; but it is a common feature of languages throughout the world. It is no easier to produce a glottal stop than an aspirated 't', so the accusation that people are being 'lazy' by using the glottal stop does not hold up. And the notion that speakers are omitting the letter 't' is also false: in their variety of English, that is simply how a 't' in that position in a word is pronounced.

For comparison, take another word: 'word'. The sound of the 'r' in 'word' can be clearly heard in many regional accents down the whole west side of Britain. Americans and Australians typically pronounce the 'r' in 'word' too. This is known as a 'rhotic' accent feature. Listen to Sir Lindsay Hoyle, Speaker of the House of Commons. He grew up in Lancashire, and you will hear the 'r' in his 'word' clearly.[11] But listen to a speaker from a more privileged, southern background – such as another prominent former member of the House of Commons, Sir Jacob Rees-Mogg – and you will hear no trace of the 'r'. The way he pronounces 'word' might be represented as 'wuhd'. Yet I have never heard Rees Mogg, or others with received pronunciation accents, being accused of poor or lazy pronunciation. And they should not be – that is simply the correct pronunciation of 'word' in their variety of English.

Deciding not to 'lose' my Lancashire accent was a personal choice. There are many in public life who have clearly made the same choice. The MP Jess Phillips, who grew up in Birmingham, has said, 'one of the things that we have to do is be able to communicate with people and actually I think my accent has been my greatest gift'.[12] Some young men in Bradford signal their membership of their Asian community by retaining distinctive Punjabi-influenced features of speech when speaking English.[13] But if someone wishes to modify their accent to join a new social group, I respect their decision. The veteran TV presenter Joan Bakewell said that having arrived at Oxford University with a Lancashire accent, she made a conscious decision one day to start speaking like the other students in her year, who had RP accents.[14] Perhaps, like the students of today surveyed by the Sutton Trust, she had been made uncomfortably aware of how she spoke. She wanted to fit in and that was one strategy for doing so. The British filmmaker and author Lucia Ritucci has described her own decision to develop a new accent by saying, 'Speaking in a posh/white accent gives me a limited sense of what privilege feels like.'[15]

A related issue is how people react to a language spoken with a 'foreign' accent. I know from experience that any French person can identify me as British the moment I say '*Bonjour*', even if they are too polite to correct my mispronunciations. Research has shown that hearing various 'foreign' accents can, as with regional accents, influence a listener's judgements about a speaker's intelligence, honesty and credibility. Accents can invoke social stereotypes of the inhabitants of different countries, as well as places within a country. Online, I have noticed tutorial services which offer to help non-native speakers of English reduce the accent that marks them as a second-language user by asking, 'Is your accent letting you down?'[16] While improving a non-native speaker's pronunciation of English could be uncontentious – if it is simply helping them become more intelligible – it should not be necessary for anyone to feel the need to mask their linguistic origins.

Similar issues of status and attitudes apply to dialects. In Britain, the dialect which is normally used in formal spoken encounters and events (and in written texts such as this book) is Standard English. We also have a range of regional and local varieties – such as Glaswegian (Glasgow), Scouse (Liverpool), Geordie (Newcastle region) – which technically come under the derogatory-sounding label of 'nonstandard' varieties. Across the globe, and contrary to popular opinion, 'nonstandard' varieties of any language do not differ from a 'standard' variety by breaking grammatical rules. Rather, they have their own grammars, and are just as systematic and internally consistent if judged by their own grammatical norms.

It is quite normal, throughout the world, for there to be a 'standard' form of a national language which is given special status, and is the variety taught to language learners abroad. But which variety becomes the standard is a matter of historical circumstances, social influences and political decisions. It is not in any meaningful way 'better' than other varieties. The locus of power in Britain, for example, has long been South-east England. Standard English is just the dialect that was, and still is, spoken by the rich and powerful. In Italy, political power has long resided in the north of the country, so standard Italian has developed from northern dialects, such as Tuscan. The language varieties spoken in southern Italy, such as Sicilian and Neapolitan, are not used for parliamentary business or to present the news on national TV.[17]

Though all dialects of any language are linguistically equal, there is no doubt that 'nonstandard' varieties are subject to misinformation and prejudice. For example, on a BBC website it says:

> **Standard English** is the form of English that is taught around the world and understood by all speakers of the language. It uses correct **grammatical rules** and can be thought of as the **formal, official**, or **polite** way of speaking or writing.
>
> **Non-standard English** is the **informal** version of the language, which can change depending on where it is being spoken.
>
> It contains lots of **slang** (very informal versions of standard words), which can be particular to a certain area or group of people, so may not be used or understood by everyone.[18]

When I read that, my heart sank – or rather my blood boiled. On the basis of what you have read so far, what do you think is wrong with those definitions? It seems that the BBC, despite its authoritative status, does not take care to be accurate about the English language. But, on the bright side, this supports the case for universal oracy education. Such gross misunderstanding would surely become less common and influential if young people learned about spoken language as a compulsory part of the school curriculum.

The way people in the UK speak English, and the kind of English they use, varies not only in terms of geography but also social class. As I grew up, I realised that people in some occupations – doctors, church ministers, lawyers – were less likely to 'talk broad', i.e. have a strong local accent or use regional dialect vocabulary. If you wanted to hear Cumbrian English, a good place to go was the livestock auction on Thursdays. But I also noticed that people – my parents, for example – sometimes changed the way they spoke depending on who they were talking to. This may be related to other social factors than class. My mother sounded far more Scottish when talking on the phone to relatives in Edinburgh than when she interacted with her English friends. As linguists describe it, she 'converged' on the accents of her conversational partners. I am sure I do that myself: do you think you do it, too?

Received pronunciation may be more immediately intelligible to a broader audience than some regional accents, and the grammar of Standard English may be more familiar, but that is simply because they have dominated mainstream media. Both the RP accent and the Standard English dialect have gained a higher status not because they are more 'correct' in any objective sense, but due to their historical links with wealth and power – and institutions like the BBC. If Lancaster had become the capital of England rather than London, we might now be hearing King Charles speaking with an accent similar to mine and people in Surrey being told that their dialect was 'nonstandard'. And language varieties continue to evolve, as do social identities. While older members of the royal family still speak with a distinctive upper-class accent, also known as 'Conservative RP', the younger generation's pronunciation is now more akin to 'Estuary English' – the accent that has become increasingly common nowadays among young people in South-east England. Differences between Standard English and regional varieties in Britain have become less marked since the 1930s, probably due to the influence of mass media and migration. As new communities of speakers have been established, new language varieties have also arisen, such as Multicultural London English, Jamaican Patois and Bengali Cockney.

A British Minister of Education once said to me, 'Why on earth would anyone want to go on speaking a "nonstandard" form of English?' I was taken aback by his apparent ignorance of the ties between varieties of language and social identities. People continue to speak local vernaculars *because* they represent the voices of their communities. The English of Newcastle's working-class neighbourhoods is as important for the identity of young people there as is the English used by Eton schoolboys. Some varieties of English may be used to demonstrate a person's membership of a particular social group. Take, for example, the relatively new English vernacular known as roadman slang, which is currently used by young people in London and some other English cities. A website for students claims, 'Mastering Roadman slang is an important part of fitting in with the youth culture of London and other urban areas.'[19]

While I was studying sociolinguistics at university, I came across the concept of 'code-switching' and I found this very helpful for making sense of my own language experiences (such as my mother's convergence towards a Scottish way of speaking on the phone). Code-switching is the way in which speakers may switch back and forth between two or more languages or language varieties.[20] Just as the character M. Jourdain in Molière's *The Bourgeois Gentleman* suddenly realises that all his life he had been 'speaking in prose and not knowing it!', I had unwittingly become a code-switcher between Standard English and my northern dialect. In doing so, I joined the majority of the global population.

All over the world, switching between a local dialect or language and a standard form is an everyday matter, and does not necessarily mean a local culture is being devalued. In Italy, for example, speakers of Sicilian are often proud, rather than ashamed, that they speak it alongside the national language. The linguist Mariagrazia De Meo has analysed the dialogue in the internationally popular TV series *Inspector Montalbano*, which is set in Sicily. She notes that, 'In the dialogue between Adelina [his housekeeper] and Montalbano . . . dialect code-switching conveys a sense of caring affection between the interlocutors'.[21] I am sure many code-switchers can relate to that sentiment. In some countries, such as India or Luxembourg, people ordinarily switch between two or three dialects or completely different languages in a day – or even within a single conversation – without any feelings of embarrassment or betrayal. They are simply socially adept speakers.

The American sociolinguist Courtney McCluney recorded a fellow researcher who grew up speaking a Black American English dialect but had learned to use Standard English, too, as saying: 'At this point in my career, code-switching feels natural. I am not even cognizant that I do it anymore.'[22] But not everyone finds it easy, or comfortable.

Code-switching can feel like a demeaning requirement imposed by a prejudiced world. If you feel you must switch codes because your natural way of talking is subject to prejudice, or unjustifiably treated as inferior, then switching into a higher status form is a forced choice. Making switches in vocabulary, style and grammar to avoid discrimination across different social situations can be demanding and stressful. Believing that you cannot speak in your authentic voice can undermine your sense of identity. It can make you feel that you cannot be your 'real self'. The American writer Allison Wiltz has argued that, for Black people like her, having to constantly adjust their ways of talking to suit white American norms 'does more harm than good'.[23] The British writer Benjamin Zephaniah, whose performance poetry drew on his Caribbean heritage, initially experienced great difficulty in having his work accepted by mainstream broadcasters and publishers.[24]

Discrimination based on language variation, as with any way of denying people respect and equality, should be challenged and resisted. It is the ignorance of listeners that should come under scrutiny and be made to change, rather than the behaviour of speakers. But just as one way to oppose racism is to expose the falseness of beliefs that underpin such attitudes and behaviour, we can hope to do the same by educating everyone about the ways spoken language naturally varies.

Whether or not any of us feel that switching codes is acceptable, then, will partly depend on why we think we are doing it. Are we doing it unwillingly, as a forced response to racism, gender bias or even snobbery? Or are we simply wanting to join a language community?

Switching codes can simply mean that a speaker is taking account of who they are conversing with: you respect your listener by addressing them in the form of language which suits the interaction, and the kind of relationship you have. Children learn how to do this through experience, as the sociolinguist Elizabeth Lanza explains, 'Learning when and when not to code-switch is an important part of *language socialization*.'[25] On my part, in conversations with friends, I use northern dialect words like 'nowt' (nothing), 'summat' (something), 'lass' (girl or woman) and 'in't it' (isn't it), which I would not use in a university conference or public presentation. I readily accept that I should not generalise from my privileged position, but personally I do not mind maintaining this distinction.

Teaching oracy could also help bidialectal or bilingual young people feel that code-switching is not necessarily identity threatening: they will know that there is no need to stop speaking their community-based 'nonstandard' English, while understanding how practically useful and rewarding it is to master more than one language variety. Zephaniah's poetry reaches a wide audience *because of* his skilful combination of Jamaican dialect and Standard English.[26] You do not have to forget English to become a Spanish speaker; and you do not have to forsake one variety of English to become a fluent speaker of another. As Qamar Shafiq, a secondary school English teacher, says:

> I spoke Punjabi at home with my parents, and spoke slang with my friends. The only opportunity I had to learn standard English was in the classroom. In fact, without an explicit focus on standard English in the classroom, I would not have even been aware of the differences between standard and non-standard English, I would often mix the two. I was clearly capable of code-switching, but as a novice learner, not very effectively![27]

The sociolinguist Ian Cushing has done important work exposing the ways in which bias against nonstandard varieties of English has permeated the reports of the English school inspection authority, Ofsted.[28] But he opposes the introduction of oracy in schools by claiming that those of us who promote it think that social injustice and inequality can be eradicated 'through marginalised children making small tweaks to their language'.[29] I do not know of anyone involved with oracy who has ever made such a claim. Injustice and inequality are systemic, and cannot be solved by the actions of individuals – especially those who are socially disadvantaged. I do not think any British child should be told they need to 'lose' their local dialect, or try to sound like a member of the privately educated elite. They should learn that RP accented Standard English is not intrinsically better than 'nonstandard' forms: it has just had the benefit of political and historical accident. The English spoken by the king is no 'more correct' than their own: it just reflects his upbringing, as their own language does for them. If they encounter anyone arguing that an upper-class accent is intrinsically superior, they can feel empowered to regard such people as bigoted. All children should, through oracy education, learn about the relationship between language, power and inequality.

But when it comes to what should happen in schools, I think Cushing is being disingenuous in his comments about educating young people about their language use. By 'making small tweaks', I take him to mean encouraging them to learn to use, in some social situations, Standard English rather than a 'nonstandard' variety. Cushing's implication is that this is pointless because it will not affect their life chances, and it would be misleading to tell them that it might make any real difference to their futures. Yet, like me, Cushing needed to speak Standard English to become an academic. How would he advise a young speaker of a local or regional dialect who wanted a similar career? I think it is misguided to insist that children who speak 'nonstandard' varieties should not be encouraged to learn more than one variety of English, or to deny that it might be important for them to modify their style of language in some situations.

The way we speak also varies in *register*, or *style* of speech. Some of us may not switch between accents and dialects, but nevertheless our talk differs depending on the situation – we 'style switch'. In formal settings, we speak differently than our informal interactions on the street. In a university committee I may use expressions like, 'One has to consider . . .', 'My proposal is . . .' or 'We face a dichotomous choice': the kind of language that I would never use in casual conversations with friends, except perhaps as a joke – 'Well, we have a dichotomous choice of real ales tonight.'

Talking and listening can affect the quality of interpersonal communication, and the impression a speaker makes. Oracy skills involve knowing what ways of talking are appropriate in different occasions. To take an extreme example, we are all likely to be aware that we should not use swear words in a court of law. Such words are not 'nonstandard' English: they exist in every language variety. And if a student swears in a classroom, this is unlikely to be due to their ignorance of social norms, but rather a deliberate, rule-breaking act of disobedience. But that student may still be glad to learn that when taking part in a recruitment interview, using a rather formal register is more likely to get them the job than the style of a casual conversation.

Oracy education would enable students to learn how to use language in ways that suit their purposes; to meet the needs of a situation and to accomplish particular tasks. They would come to appreciate that a team of scientists might discuss a project in language that would be unintelligible to a non-scientist, but that this is simply a specialised and efficient mode of communication, which allows them to effectively work together as a team. Science education should make students fluent speakers of science.[30] And we should only decry that kind of language as 'jargon' if the scientists relied on it when trying to explain their project to the general public.

Upon entering school, most children quickly become aware that the formal language of schooling has its own expressions, words and rules. They may need help to realise that being academically successful *and* maintaining relationships in the playground means using a range of speech styles. If they hope to go into higher education, this will inevitably require the use of Standard English grammar, and of an 'academic register'. However, most schools currently provide no guidance or instruction on how to develop an academic vocabulary and style. Very few young people are expressly taught how to present themselves in interviews, how to take part in productive discussions, or how to use the technical languages of different subjects. They are just expected to pick that up as they go along. Deciding if and when to change your accent, dialect or register should be a well-informed personal choice, based on knowledge about language in its social context. Simply changing the way you speak will not open all the doors to opportunity, but becoming adept at coping with the demands of social communication will make opportunities more likely and encounters more rewarding.

Oracy education will enable people to broaden their linguistic repertoire, not 'stamp out' their nonstandard or slang usage. It cannot eliminate social disadvantage, but it can help to give young people a voice and to challenge the systems that support linguistic discrimination. It will help them recognise and resist unwarranted judgements about the way they speak. Opposing efforts to help young people learn to speak confidently and effectively in different social situations – and by implication leave oracy skills to the rich and privileged – is therefore dangerously defeatist.

In his *Teacherhead* blog, the British secondary school teacher Tom Sherrington recalls hearing a student reporting in a school assembly about a school trip that he had greatly enjoyed:

> This was an occasion where a formal speech code would have been appropriate, not least because he was a significant role-model. Throughout his speech he used 'done': 'We done a trek; we done a trip to the market; we done a presentation' . . . My instinct was that, since he had been in that school for six years, we should have

> done a better job in teaching him the formal speech code that would have led him to say, 'we went on a trek; we gave a presentation' and so on. My sense is that, without that fluency and self-awareness, this student will be undermined and undeservedly disempowered in the real world where formal speech carries significant value. Is that wrong?
>
> It was also my strong feeling that a major reason this student had not yet fully mastered appropriate formal speech was that [his] . . . teachers had been reluctant to address the issue on a day-to-day basis for fear of being insensitive or denigrating his default speech mode. I discussed it with him explicitly – because he had interviews to prepare for. He saw it as a failing of his education that he hadn't been taught to 'speak well' – as he put it – even when he wanted to and he was concerned that the habits were now hard to break.[31]

From this account, it seems the boy's teachers felt they faced a dilemma. On the one hand, they thought they should not tell students to stop using their usual vernacular style, because to do so would be discourteous. On the other hand, they knew that there were good reasons for encouraging students to change the way they talked in some situations, if they wanted to leave the desired impression. Fortunately, Sherrington realised that this apparent dilemma is based on a false dichotomy: no hard choice needs to be made between speaking Standard English and speaking a regional variety. His student did not have to stop using the English variety he had grown up with, but it might help him to negotiate a range of social interactions more confidently and successfully if he also learned to use the standard variety and socially appropriate registers. Through providing knowledge about spoken language, oracy education can offer both teachers and students the solution.

Language is part of our culture: it links us to our roots. We all should learn about the histories and characteristics of the kinds of spoken language that exist within our society; how speech differs from writing; the ways language needs to be adapted to pursue different tasks; and how and why, within any society, ways of speaking are commonly linked to prejudice and injustice. Nobody should feel ashamed of the language they have grown up with: it can be a proud part of their identity. But everyone can be encouraged to acquire new languages, varieties, vocabularies and registers in order to become a better communicator. If oracy became an intrinsic component of the curriculum, it could enable all students to develop their communication skills and to underpin those skills with a sound understanding of how spoken language works.

5. Speaking in Public

A 2023 survey in the UK reported that 57 per cent of women and 39 per cent of men find the prospect of addressing a room full of people frightening.[1] This is far from surprising; unless they were privately educated, British people are unlikely to have had any oracy instruction in this task. Public speaking is far less daunting if you are taught how best to convey ideas, how to gain and hold an audience's attention, and how to persuade them not only to believe you, but to believe *in* you.

It is perhaps to be expected, then, that a disproportionate number of private school alumni are elected politicians. In 2024, less than 6 per cent of the British adult population were privately educated. Even after the election of a Labour government that same year, which brought the proportion of privately educated MPs down to an all-time low, they still constituted 23 per cent of Parliament. In 2023, 65 per cent of senior judges in the UK and 45 per cent of the highest-paid BBC radio and TV presenters were privately educated.[2] There are other reasons for this disparity, of course: privilege provides many routes to power. But the lack of oracy education in state schools is an obstacle to everyone's active participation in democratic society.

Teaching oracy should improve the representation of the general population in public life. Developing the ability and confidence to address meetings will enable less privileged people to resist oppression and to fight for social justice. Public-speaking skills are of course also valuable for pursuing careers currently dominated by former private school students, such as law, acting and broadcast journalism. Oracy education could not create open access to those professions, but it could embolden a wider range of applicants. While there are several organisations in the UK that offer relevant, accessible public-speaking training to young people from all social backgrounds, such as the English-Speaking Union, the Speakers Trust and Debate Mate, these inevitably only reach and benefit a relative few.[3]

One specialised form of public speaking is formal debate. Debating has a long and esteemed history across time and cultures, as a type of dialogue for allowing arguments to be put forward and challenged, often in a formal setting. Debating is all about justifying a point of view to an audience and convincing them of your case. It is a special kind of contest in which speakers also challenge propositions made by others, and sometimes there is a moderator who ensures all voices are heard. As with many aspects of culture in the UK, ranging from ballet to cricket, it seems that debate has largely been associated with the middle and upper classes. Former private school students are disproportionally represented in the Oxford Union, which claims to be 'the most prestigious debating society in the world'.[4] But debate should not be defined by what happens in such places: formal argumentation also has deep roots in campaigns for women's suffrage and working-class politics. One consequence of the suppression of the UK trade union movement is that it has reduced the opportunities for working-class people to develop their public-speaking and oracy skills through active participation in collective discussion. Trade unions launched the successful parliamentary careers of British MPs such as John Prescott and Angela Rayner. Rayner was encouraged by her workmates to represent them because, she says, 'I was mouthy and would take no messing from management.'[5]

At public-speaking competitions, I have been pleased to find that competitors are increasingly drawn from state schools – and proportionally there are many more girls. However, from what teachers tell me, it seems that most come from middle-class families. There is still a need to convince all young people that such activities are not the preserve of the privileged. My colleagues and I have worked with state schools that have set up 'parliaments', debating societies and discussion groups. In their excellent book *Transform Teaching and Learning*

Through Talk, Amy Gaunt and Alice Stott (of Voice 21) argue that 'the skill of debating comes down to *having* to think of arguments and counterarguments. This process forces students to engage with perspectives they may not have otherwise considered, and their opinion may shift as a result.'[6]

Some forms of public speaking do not have the same class connotations. A teacher in a south London secondary school told me that some of his students would be extremely reluctant to make a formal speech to an assembly, but would have no such fears about performing an impromptu rap to a similar sized audience. The oracy skills needed for such a performance are at least as demanding as those required for debating. Similarly, stand-up comedy is not strongly associated with upper-class culture. But as Sian Davies, a comedian from Liverpool says, 'Being working class is a real barrier in the comedy industry, where the privately educated continue to dominate the top tier.'[7] The main obstacle seems to be financial, with wealthier comedians being able to support themselves through the Bank of Mum and Dad. Such support can, of course, also fund extracurricular improvisation classes. Sian adds: 'While there is still a long way to go, the industry has schemes in place for diversity and equality when it comes to gender, disability, race and sexuality. But there is nothing when it comes to class.'

I am often asked if it is appropriate to propose that all students be taught how to speak in public. If you are naturally shy, say, should you be made to do something that feels so stressful? Teachers have told me that some parents have objected to their children being given an oracy education, because being asked to speak in public will upset them. But you do not have to be an extrovert to be an effective public speaker. Some of the most effective speakers are not party people. While it would be wrong to force anyone into a situation which makes them extremely anxious, I think it is unfortunate if young people are not offered the opportunity to overcome their fears. It is patronising to assume that the quiet child does not wish to speak, or even has nothing to say.

So far, I have talked about public speaking in terms of addressing a large audience, while standing at the front, alone. But of course, for a child at school, public speaking may simply be speaking in front of their classmates. What might seem to be a small step is enough to make many children stumble at the first hurdle, so to speak; some will not talk in class for all the years they attend school. The conditions will have to be right. Teachers need to ensure that every child knows that there will be no adverse consequences to speaking up. The key is to create an environment in which every child feels that their voice is valued.[8] The ability to take part in a debate or give a speech is within most people's grasp and can readily be taught. The kind of guidance and instruction that can be offered is a far cry from the elocution lessons that I avoided in my youth, which seemed principally to be designed to iron out regional accents.

The skills for public speaking, as set out in the Oracy Skills Framework, can be considered, described, exemplified, rehearsed, practised and put to use. You don't have to be born a great orator: the best way to become a fluent and self-assured public speaker is to learn. And doing so can take account of who you are; we should not all aim to sound the same. Encouraging fluency does not mean discriminating against people who stammer:[9] it means enabling anyone to learn how to communicate effectively. Performers do not need to be supremely confident, but they need to *appear* confident to their audience, and comfortably connect with their audience. These are skills in themselves, learned through practice.

The ancient Greeks identified specific ways that speakers could engage and persuade their audiences. These are known as *rhetorical devices* or *techniques*.[10] One technique that can stimulate audience applause is the *contrast*. This can be found in John F. Kennedy's appeal to Americans: 'Ask not what your country can do for you, ask what you can do for your country.'

Other effective rhetorical devices are:

1. The three point list:

   'Government of the people, by the people, for the people.'

   'Our priorities are education, education, education.'

2. Repetition of key words:

   'Nature is not just wildlife; nature is not just something we see outside; nature is the foundation for all our lives.'

3. Rhetorical questions:

   'If you prick us, do we not bleed? If you tickle us, do we not laugh?'

4. Summaries:

   'So the main points I have made are . . . '

Such devices only come alive in the context of real speeches. When we were creating the Oracy Skills Framework, my colleagues and I went to School 21 to see oracy in action with classes of eleven-year-olds, many of whom had experienced social deprivation. At the start of the school year, I watched a teacher organising the class into groups of eight students. Each student then gave a brief two-minute talk to their group on a topic they had chosen. Afterwards, group members and the teacher responded with helpful feedback and suggestions (which could include proposing they try using one of the rhetorical devices listed above). The aim was for students to eventually address a whole class or school meeting; something which would be too difficult, initially, for most of them. I learned that this was the first stage of oracy training the teachers had developed for their 'Ignite Talks' held in the summer term, in which: 'Every student in the year gives a five-minute speech (without notes) on a subject close to their heart, accompanied by 20 slides. Writing and rehearsing the talks, deciding on which tones of voice to use, what body language and so on is the key work in Oracy lessons for Year 7. This is a real challenge to their abilities to work together, discuss, debate and agree a workable end-product which they then perform to the assembled school community.'[11] And the end of year performance involves the whole school community including parents.

The principal elements of the kind of public speaking education that School 21 was providing for its Year 7 students can be summed up as follows:

- Begin teaching students in a safe, contained situation: for example, start with a group of 6–8 students who, with the teacher, listen to each other's presentations.

- Offer students a range of topics to talk about. Suggest that they choose a subject with which they feel confident (they may have their own suggestions).
- Suggest ways in which students can make their speeches effective: for example, by including a three-point list or concluding with a summary.
- Give students plenty of time to prepare. Ask them to work on their ideas with a classmate. Use rehearsals and build up confidence with mutual supportive feedback.
- Students can have a list of key words as prompts but should not read their presentation.
- Ask each student to present for a **maximum of two minutes** initially.
- Ensure that students know how to be a good audience, attending to the speaker and being ready to provide supportive and constructive feedback to their classmates.

Young people who have taken part in such programmes are ready to acknowledge the benefits; such as these Year 9 students in a British comprehensive secondary school who said, 'It's taught me to stand up for myself and that what I want to say is important. I have found my voice'; 'I learnt how to stand up in front of a big group of people confidently';[12] 'Now I have the courage to speak in all of my classes.' In the 2023 report on the impact of their work with schools, the charity Voice 21 quoted a sixth-former saying: 'In Year 7, I was a quiet person. I was so scared. But now, my oracy skills have helped me to become Deputy Head Girl.'[13]

Helping students to become good public speakers will of course mean focusing on learning *how to* talk; but for them to appreciate how and why good speakers are effective, they will need to learn *about* talk, too. One method is to study the speeches of prominent orators, from Steve Jobs and Barack Obama to Margaret Thatcher and Greta Thunberg. Consider, for example, Thunberg's use of repetition and the three-point list:

> You have stolen my dreams and my childhood with your empty words. And yet I'm one of the lucky ones. People are suffering. People are dying. Entire ecosystems are collapsing. We are in the beginning of a mass extinction, and all you can talk about is money and fairy tales of eternal economic growth. How dare you![14]

Students can first be asked to share their initial emotional reactions to a speech, and next to share their more considered responses to its content. They can then, with their teacher, go on to analyse its structure and the rhetorical techniques. In that way they can understand better how the speaker achieved their impact.

After older students have gained a deeper understanding of public speaking, it can be valuable to look at unconventional oratory successes, too. A case in point is Donald Trump. As he grew in prominence on the political stage, I heard many people, typically those who did not share his views, describe him as an incoherent speaker who often contradicted himself and made wild, unsubstantiated claims. There is no doubt that Trump's speeches score high on self-aggrandisement and low on truthfulness. He is not succinct and often seems to wander off topic. Yet Trump is highly effective in building a rapport with, and enthusing, his followers. Any politician who can persuade over 76 million Americans to vote for him, and who receives such powerful receptions at his rallies, must be doing something right. It is important to avoid any initial judgements and to ask questions about his use of spoken English, such as:

- What rhetorical techniques does he use?
- What particular features make his speeches so distinctive?
- Why do his speeches appeal so strongly to his target audience, and why are they so effective in getting a positive response?

It might seem that Trump's style is strikingly opposed to that of a classical rhetorician; bluster and bombast as opposed to eloquent entreaty. But he relies heavily on two related ancient Greek techniques:[15]

- *epistrophe* – the repetition of a word or expression at the end of successive phrases or sentences:

  'We have to find out what is the problem; and we do have a problem, believe me.'

  'Go back eight weeks. I want to go back eight weeks. Let's go back eight weeks.'

- *anaphora* – the repetition of a word or phrase near the beginning of successive clauses or sentences:

  'We will be prosperous, we will be proud, we will be strong, and we will win like never before.'

  'We're going to help our country heal. We have a country that needs help, and it needs help very badly. We're going to fix our borders, we're going to fix everything about our country . . . '

Trump also has his own distinctive ways with words that differentiates him from most other successful American politicians. He frequently addresses his audience as 'you'; he explicitly appeals for support from 'the silent majority', by which he means the blue-collar cohort of American voters who feel disenfranchised. He defines himself as the defender of ordinary Americans against external enemies.[16]

The linguist Dr Jennifer Sclafani has suggested his style comes more from the tradition of salesmanship than politics.[17] The commentator Evan Puschak, who posts online as The Nerdwriter, agrees, saying that 'as a lifelong salesman, [Trump] has a huckster's knack for selling a feeling'. He has a bank of catchphrases and 'buzzwords' which he uses to appeal to his loyal audience's shared history of his speeches ('Lock her up!', 'Fake news', 'Believe me'. He used the word 'hoax' more than 250 times in speeches in 2020). At rallies, his audiences commonly echo and chant these words after Trump has said them. In that way – similar to the 'call-and-response' routines of evangelical preachers with their congregations – he uses language as a tool to strengthen the bonds between him and his community. Trump also makes religious references, for example appeals to God, far more often than any previous president.[18] And unlike many politicians, Trump often makes his audience laugh. But an analysis of his speeches has shown that they have come to contain much more violent language over recent years.[19]

Trump always employs lots of one-syllable words and avoids the extended metaphors so beloved of other politicians. A study carried out by the *Boston Globe* put speeches by Trump, Hillary Clinton and Bernie Sanders through the Flesch-Kincaid Reading Test, used to assess the level of reading comprehension needed to understand a text.[20] It seems that while a speech by Sanders would require the comprehension skills of the average 10th Grade (Year 11) student, Trump's speeches only require those of a 4th Grader (Year 5). Clinton's speeches came between those two.

What can we – and students of public speaking – learn from studying Trump? We can see how he can captivate his audience. He uses both classical rhetorical techniques and his own, quirky stylistic features. His distinctive register has convinced many voters that although he is a rich, white, New York businessman, he is not a member of the metropolitan, 'liberal' elite that they distrust. They hear him speaking like 'one of them', not an Ivy League 'lawmaker'. His way of talking creates a shared vocabulary that his community can use to voice their fears and aspirations. And while spoken language is not the sole reason why any politician succeeds or fails, the event that precipitated Biden's withdrawal as a presidential candidate was his poor performance in a televised debate with Trump.

For comparison, we might consider the oratory of Sir

Keir Starmer. A very different kind of politician from Trump, Starmer does not favour a highly emotional style of delivery, and maintains more detachment from his audience. But he also makes use of established rhetorical techniques. For example, in one of his first speeches after being elected in August 2024, he employed both *anaphora* (the emphatic repetition of an initial word or phrase) and the three-part list:

> This shouldn't be a country where the Prime Minister can't guarantee prison places. This shouldn't be a country where people are paying thousands more on their mortgage. Or waiting months for hospital appointments they desperately need. Where our waters are filled with sewage. Where parents worry that their kids won't get the opportunities they did. Where nothing seems to work anymore.[21]

Whether Starmer's political rhetoric will ensure continued support from the British electorate remains an open question. From oracy education, young people can begin to understand how politicians and others on the public stage use talk to appeal to their audiences. Such knowledge can underpin the development of their own spoken language skills, through raising their awareness of how the spoken word can influence people to think and act in certain ways. It can also enable them to become more critical of what they hear in the public domain, and so perhaps more able to distinguish a weak argument from a strong one, truth from falsehood, and rhetorical appeals to anger rather than to reason. Of course, it could also help them to become powerful persuaders themselves, in the pursuit of good or evil; oracy skills can be employed to further any cause. But if we are serious about creating societies in which there is widespread participation in democracy, and access to the 'speaking professions' is not limited to the children of the most affluent, then education policy needs to prioritise oracy.

6. Collaboration

Despite the popular image of the lone genius, most important discoveries and creations are the products of collaboration, from the specification of the DNA double helix to the music of the Beatles. The fact that Britain 'punches above its weight' in gaining Nobel Prizes for science has been explained by an academic tradition of establishing research units, which bring together people who are doing exciting things so that they can talk and work together.[1] (Though that does not only happen in Britain, of course.)

The same kind of explanation is relevant to the arts, too. Authorship might seem like a solitary endeavour. However, some masterpieces of Romantic literature, for example, were the result of collaborations between writers such as Mary Shelley and Percy Bysshe Shelley, or Samuel Taylor Coleridge and William Wordsworth.[2] The psychologist Vera John-Steiner has argued that truly transformative thinking – for example, that which results in the creation of new art forms – is commonly the result of a shared visionary commitment to change being pursued by people working closely together.[3]

In 2016, the World Economic Forum stated that in today's world of work, young people 'must be adept at collaboration, communication and problem-solving'.[4] In 2015, the UK Commission for Employment and Skills reported that there was a shortage of skills in customer handling, oral/written communication, problem-solving and working effectively with others in a team.[5] In 2015, the OECD said:

> Collaborative problem solving is increasingly recognised as an important 21st century skill as it has several advantages over individual problem solving: labour can be divided equally, a variety of perspectives and experiences can be applied to try and find solutions, and team members can support and stimulate one another, in turn enhancing the creativity and quality of solutions.[6]

Collaborating is one of the most important things we do, yet many of us have experienced badly run, time-consuming meetings which seem to go awry and produce little of value. Two or more heads are often much better than one, but highly qualified, capable people can also end up wasting each other's time.

We must try to ensure the success of collaborative efforts: the difficulties we face in the world today will only be solved if we optimise our efforts for thinking together. It is therefore vital to provide young people with an education that will improve the quality of their ability to interthink.

In the world of work, stressful, unproductive meetings can be demoralising. In her book *Conversational Intelligence*, which is about the effective use of talk in business settings, the leadership coach Judith Glaser includes a section called 'The worst conversations at work'.[7] Before she began to coach a particular corporate leader, she asked members of his team what they thought about the ways he chaired meetings. One said: 'We feel like kids at an elementary school with a horrible teacher redlining our work.' When asked what they thought could improve their meetings, staff said: 'Just for once, he should ask us what *we* think, or what *we* want to talk about, or what's on *our* minds.' I expect that will resonate with many people's experiences.

But let's look on the positive side. I want you to think back to when you have been working with a group of people – three or more. A staff meeting perhaps, in which you had to plan some action or reach a decision. Choose an occasion when you think it went well. What characterises a successful collaboration? What would you see and hear happening that would tell you that people were working well together – that it was a *good discussion*? Make a list, and we will come back to it shortly.

Back in the 1960s, the psychologist Irving Janis sought to explain why powerful organisations of apparently intelligent people made disastrous decisions.[8] He took as his example the US government's decision to continue the Vietnam War in the 1960s, when most well-informed people could see no good reason for doing so. Janis suggested that this was because those involved succumbed to a phenomenon he called 'groupthink'. When decision makers were under pressure, they prioritised maintaining solidarity within the group, instead of encouraging critical dissent. They stopped listening to 'outsiders' and dismissed ideas that threatened the status quo. Their discussions were conducted in ways not conducive to finding the best solutions. That is, they seemed to follow unwritten social rules, including:

1. Do not express arguments against the group's majority view.
2. Do not invoke any views or evidence which might undermine consensus.
3. Do not question the judgement of a senior colleague.
4. Provide support rather than criticism.
5. Use any opportunities to express support for the official group stance.

In 2024, political commentators offered a similar analysis as to why Joe Biden and his close supporters resisted, for so long, the calls for him to withdraw his presidential candidacy.[9] When interthinking was required, what happened instead was groupthink. To avoid groupthink, Janis suggested raising awareness of it among those in power; and using constructive techniques, such as one or more members acting as a 'devil's advocate' when crucial issues were being debated. However, we can do more to make collective decision-making robust.

The emergence of groupthink is an extreme example of how implicit social rules can shape the nature of group activity; preventing the kind of critical, rational dialogue needed for successful problem-solving. The key to achieving more productive discussion lies in the implementation of a different set of social rules. This can be illustrated through the American law courts. Back in 2020, Judge Sonia Sotomayor was identified as the US Supreme Court judge who was most frequently interrupted during the previous year's court cases, in research carried out by Tonja Jacobi and Dylan Schweers of Northwestern University.[10] They found that 'judicial interactions at oral argument were highly gendered, with women interrupted at disproportionate rates by male colleagues and male advocates'. They suggested that the most senior female judges only coped by 'learning over time to behave more like male justices'. As Sotomayor herself put it, 'I respond in a way which perhaps I shouldn't, which is: I interrupt back.'

Sotomayor's more considered solution was to introduce a new format for how debates in court were conducted, so that opportunities for interruptions would be limited. In other words, she changed the 'ground rules'. The original use of this term was in sport, referring to rules that are not written in the official rule book, but which players need to follow – for example, while most golf courses allow golf buggies to be wheeled everywhere, on the Old Course at St Andrews, the birthplace of golf, visiting players are expected to keep to designated paths. The term is now commonly applied to implicit social norms. Some speaking and listening activities do have explicit rules – for example, debating contests. But most of the spoken interactions in our lives have no rulebooks. We have to pick up the unspoken, cultural norms in order to make social situations conform to expectations and ensure that things go smoothly. For example, at job interviews, the interviewers need to know that they are expected to ask the questions and direct the proceedings; the candidates need to know that they are expected to answer and not run the show. Nobody gets handed a rule book before the event begins. But an important ground rule is to 'answer all questions as politely and as fully as necessary'. If a candidate refuses to, or if they announce, 'I think I'll ask all the questions today', they would be breaking the ground rules and the interview would probably fall apart, and that candidate is unlikely to be recruited.

If you look beneath the surface, you will see that all interactions are governed by ground rules, some of which may be helpful and some of which are not. Revealing them can be the first step towards better practice. One of the best professional development courses I ever attended was called 'fair selection training'. Its aim was to make job recruitment in the university not only fairer but more effective at selecting the best candidates. Through video, role-play and guidance, we were encouraged to critically examine the ways that interviews often unfolded, to try asking different kinds of questions and listen more carefully to answers that candidates gave. I thought I knew more than most people about spoken language, but the course radically changed the way I carried out that important aspect of my work.

Many kinds of situations require skilled talk management. The behaviour of a media interviewer can make all the difference to whether an interviewee relaxes and speaks freely, or whether they feel they are unjustifiably under attack and clam up. In my experience, medical practitioners have become far better at listening to patients, and explaining things in a jargon-free way. This can be attributed to many medical students now receiving relevant oracy training. However, in her 2024 book *Unheard: The medical practice of silencing*, the British doctor Rageshri Dhairyawan argues that more attention still needs to be given to developing listening skills if patients are to be treated properly. [11] I do not think it is an exaggeration to say that the quality of many people's lives could be improved significantly if more priority was given to making us all better interpersonal communicators.

Let's consider another form of talk with a different kind of purpose: getting to know someone at a dinner or party. The sociolinguist Deborah Tannen researched such social gatherings, and found that misunderstandings could arise about what behaviour was deemed appropriate if participants had different cultural backgrounds.[12] A Thanksgiving party she organised in New York was attended by two male friends who were, like Tannen, New Yorkers, and three other guests: two Californian men and an English woman. From Tannen's perspective as host, the evening seemed to go well. When she asked her fellow New Yorkers how they thought it had gone, they said that they had also found the conversation lively and satisfying. But feedback from the other guests was less favourable. They said they felt threatened by the intense pace of the conversation and the constant barrage of questions about their personal lives from the New Yorkers. They did not feel it appropriate to enquire after intrusive details. In other words, the New Yorkers seemed to abide by the conversational ground rules below:

- Ask people direct questions about their personal lives, interests, occupations and so on as it shows that you are interested in getting to know them.
- Share personal details of your own life as it shows that you trust the people you are with.
- Interrupt speakers if you have something urgent to say about what they have said as it shows that you really are interested.

If Tannen's other guests were suitable cultural representatives, it seems that those conversational ground rules were at odds with those that would apply in England or California. As an English person, I think they were. I have a cherished example of conflicting conversational ground rules from my own experience. It comes from when a Dutch friend stayed in my home. The citizens of the Netherlands are known to be straight talkers. My wife and I were talking about replacing an orange table lamp which had a 1960s style that I particularly liked. She agreed it was distinctive, but felt its time had come and gone. Our Dutch friend was asked for his opinion. 'It is horrible!' he said without hesitation. I don't think a British visitor would have been so forthright. We replaced the lamp (and we are all still friends).

In several classroom-based studies, my colleagues and I have analysed the talk of children working together in groups of three on a task set by the teacher, but without the teacher present.[13] We compared the features of productive discussions, in which participants completed the task successfully, with group discussions that had less positive outcomes. We found that participants in the more productive discussions seemed to implicitly follow ground rules such as 'everyone should contribute', 'give reasons for your views', 'respectfully challenge any ideas you think are wrong' and 'strive for agreement'.

Do any of those ground rules sound familiar? I hope so, because it is the cue for you to return to the list you made earlier. Essentially, we found that the best, most productive discussions were those in which students did the following things:

- all actively participated
- shared relevant information
- engaged critically but constructively with each other's ideas
- gave reasons for their ideas
- checked understanding by asking questions
- built on each other's responses
- strove for agreement

They also used significantly more expressions and words linked to reasoning, such as 'I think', 'because' and 'if'. We called this kind of dialogue 'Exploratory Talk', a term first coined by the pioneering classroom researcher

Douglas Barnes.[14] How closely do the defining characteristics of Exploratory Talk match your ideas of a useful and engaging discussion?

Other discussions among groups of students seemed to be based on ground rules that did not generate productive outcomes. Some were reminiscent of groupthink, such as: 'if someone is your friend, always agree with them'. In those groups, students might share ideas, but they did not pick up or build upon each other's contributions. It seemed they were following the rule: 'just say what you think, don't ask anyone else for their thoughts'. Some students seemed minimally involved and there was little collaborative reasoning. Although group relations were not tense or hostile, these discussions were not very creative or productive. We called this 'Cumulative Talk'.

There were also group discussions of a very different kind, rather like those I mentioned in US law courts, seemingly based on rules like: 'interrupt a speaker immediately if they say something with which you disagree'. Some even resembled televised political debates, in which a speaker's main aim seemed to be just to oppose any alternative point of view and 'put down' other speakers. Participants also seemed to follow rules such as: 'just stick to your original point of view, whatever anyone says' and 'if you think someone's idea is stupid, say so'. We called this kind of discussion 'Disputational Talk'. Here's an example from two ten-year-old girls who are meant to be writing a dialogue together for cartoon characters:

Carol:	Just write in the next letter. 'Did you have a nice English lesson?' (*Jo typing on computer.*)
Jo:	You've got to get it on there. Yes, that's you. Let's just have a look at that. 'Hi Alan, did you have a nice English lesson? Yes, thank you, yeah. Yes, thank you, it was fine.'
Carol:	You've got to let me get some in sometimes.
Jo:	You're typing.
Carol:	Well, you can do some, go on.
Jo:	'Yes, thank you.'
Carol:	(*Mumbles*)
Jo:	You're typing. 'Yes, thank you', 'I did, yeah, yes, thank you, I did.'
Carol:	You can spell that.
Jo:	Why don't you do it?
Carol:	No, because you should.

Carol and Jo seem to treat each other more as an adversary than a collaborator. Like many adults engaged in unproductive discussions, they were probably unaware of how their conversational behaviour affected the success of their joint enterprise. Overall, we found that Cumulative Talk and Disputational Talk occurred a lot in classrooms, while Exploratory Talk happened much less often. This helps to explain why some teachers have claimed that groupwork is a waste of time. Tom Bennett, the prominent educational 'influencer', has written: 'Group work: I hate the concept, as I hate hell, all Montagues and thee. I bite my thumb at it . . . An efficient way to learn? Not so much.'[15] Also on social media, secondary history teacher Robert Peal, wrote: 'whenever I am asked where the group work is in my lessons, I respond with the same answer. The class have been put into a group of 30, and their group task is to listen to the teacher and to work in silence'.[16] Yet if groupwork is not productive in a teacher's classroom, this is the fault of the teacher, not their students. And this is a great shame, as well-organised group work improves academic attainment.[17]

Simply giving students opportunities to talk doesn't guarantee effective collaboration, because most of them may not know how to use talk to work well together. They may also let various factors, such as their feelings towards other group members, shape how they behave. They are almost certainly following some inappropriate ground rules – but if their teacher has not alerted them to this, how can they be expected to behave differently? Students are being expected to carry on a reasoned discussion, but they may rarely encounter such dialogue in their lives. Why should they be expected to know how to do it in school? They need to be *taught* how to work in groups. Students are taught other kinds of problem-solving behaviour before their teacher expects them to do it successfully. I can't imagine any teacher saying, 'I asked my students to do long division and gave them some problems to solve. But they got nowhere. So I'm giving up on long division now.'

A teacher needs to get students to agree to follow the most useful ground rules. Here are five steps to establish the right conditions for productive groupwork in the classroom:

Step 1: Raise students' awareness of how they talk and work together; think together about the importance of talk and what impact talk has on thinking.

Step 2: Ask students about their experiences of working in groups. Do they like working together? When do things go right or wrong?

Step 3: With some guidance from the teacher (who is familiar with Exploratory Talk), get students to agree on a set of ground rules which they will follow when working together.[18]

Step 4: Create some suitable collaborative group work tasks for them to practise using these rules.

Step 5. Regularly review progress with the whole class, stressing the links between speaking, listening, thinking and learning.

And here is a set of ground rules which a teacher established with her Year 6 class:

1. Everyone should have a chance to talk.
2. Everyone's ideas should be carefully considered.
3. Each member of the group should be asked:
   What do you think?
   Why do you think that?
4. Look at and listen to the person talking.
5. After discussing, agree together what to do.

You will see that this is essentially a definition of Exploratory Talk, written in child-friendly language.

As part of Step 3 in the first list of steps above, the teacher put these ground rules up on the wall; and in Step 4, referred to it when she was setting up group activities. We can see Step 5 in action in this teacher-led whole-class discussion in a primary school, in which they are reviewing their talk activities:

Teacher: OK, as I'm wandering around the classroom and looking and watching and listening to what you are doing, I wonder what sort of things I might hear you saying? Go on. Tell your partner one thing you might say. Bernice, can you tell Sydney? And . . . stop! Ready? Looking this way. Donal's group. Share one of the things I might hear you say.

Donal: What do you think?

Teacher: 'What do you think?' Brilliant – Emma?

Emma: Why do you think that?

Teacher: 'Why do you think that?' That's another good one, not just what but why do you think that? Brilliant. Anything else I might hear you saying as I wander round? Joe?

Joe: Yes and no.

Teacher: 'Yes and no'. OK. People agreeing and disagreeing. Would you expand on just saying 'yes' or would you expand on just saying 'no'?

Anna: You'd say why.

Teacher: 'Yes' and then 'why'.

In some ways, this is a very traditional kind of classroom dialogue. The teacher checks that her class know what to do when they begin their activity by asking them some 'closed' questions, which require 'right answers'. But through this conventional process, she prepares them for working collaboratively and independently without her intervention. Hearing their answers helps her feel confident that they have learned how to use talk to pursue their task.

Through a series of research projects, mainly in the UK and Mexico,[19] we have found that if students agree to follow the ground rules, and are given good opportunities to practise using them, they start to collaborate much more effectively over time. Here is an example from a discussion by some Year 6 children who had gone through the five steps with their teacher. They had to predict how many sheets of paper would completely obscure a light source:

Ross: OK. (*Reads*) 'Talk together about a plan to test all the different types of paper.'

Alana: Dijek, how much did you think it would be for tissue paper?

Dijek: At least ten because tissue paper is thin. Tissue paper can wear out and you can see through it . . . and light can shine through it.

Alana: OK. Thanks. (*To Ross)* Why do you think it?

Ross: Because I tested it before!

Alana: No, Ross, what did you think? How much did you think? Tissue paper. How much tissue paper did you think it would be to block out the light?

Ross: At first I thought it would be five, but second . . .

Alana: Why did you think that?

Ross: Because when it was in the overhead projector you could see a little bit of it, but not all of it, so I thought it would be, like, five to block out the light.

Alana: That's a good reason. I thought, I thought it would be between five and seven because, I thought it would be between five and seven because normally when you're at home if you lay it on top, with one sheet you can see through but if you lay on about five or six pieces on top you can't see through.

This extract was typical of their whole discussion. Members of the group asked each other for opinions. They all joined in. They exchanged reasons – notice their uses of 'why?', 'because', 'if' and 'so'. They evaluated any proposals that were made. They listened to each other and acknowledged the value of what was said. They worked towards an agreed conclusion. Opinions were treated with respect, and each speaker had the opportunity to develop their ideas. To make Exploratory Talk and educationally valuable groupwork happen, students were using the relevant skills from the Oracy Skills Framework.

We know that teachers appreciate the improvement in the quality of groupwork that oracy brings. But what do students think about learning in this way? My colleague Topsy Page has asked primary school children about adopting the ground rules for Exploratory Talk,[20] and their warm responses have included: 'We work together. When the other partner talks, you wait for them to finish', 'There is a big difference. It's changed a lot – we agree and disagree with each other more now' and 'Instead of me saying "You're wrong", which could make them feel upset and they'll think they're dumb, I can say, "I'd like to respectfully disagree with your opinion". Then they'll know you're not trying to be mean. They'll feel more safe.'

Secondary physics teacher Ollie Lovell writes online

regularly about his experiences in the classroom.[21] He used the ground rules approach with his Year 11 students when they were working together on electrical circuits. He then asked the students what they thought. One said: 'When we followed the rules we worked faster, communication was much better . . . less silliness, so the work was better. So like now, the first half hour, they were only doing the first one and they can't do it, then when they just followed the rules . . . we just finish like three circuits in like half an hour. So I think, the good thing about this is much work, good communication, more team work.' Lovell's own conclusion was: 'The quality of the discussions really went up a notch, students were asking many more "why" questions and planning more thoroughly before just plugging in circuit components and flicking the switch on. But the thing that surprised me the most was the impact it had on their ability to collectively problem solve.'

We have systematically tested these conclusions by observing what happens when students are educated in how to work well in a group, and by comparing what happens in classrooms where no such guidance is provided. The transformation may take up to about ten weeks, but it is often striking. We know that following the right ground rules can, over such a relatively short time, become second nature for students, and their groupwork becomes much more productive and enjoyable.

We have found this with students as young as five and as old as fifteen. Here are some other comments that young people have made about working together in this structured way:

- 'Talk partners help us help each other.' (Age 7)
- 'You need to use other people's brains. They talk, you talk and you try to link it together.' (Age 10)
- 'There used to be some people talking all the time and other people never opening their mouths. Now we hear what everyone thinks and the work gets done!' (Age 12)[22]

For young people whose out-of-school lives have given them little exposure to rational discussion, to *reasoned dialogue*, this can be a life-changing experience. They not only become able to work better together in class, but also acquire valuable skills for beyond school. They are not only learning *how to* talk together more productively, they are learning *about* their use of talk as a toolkit for interthinking, and, as a result, they learn *through* talk more effectively.

Other researchers have supported this approach. A team at the UCL Institute of Education, led by Rose Luckin, published a report in 2016 on collective problem-solving in classrooms.[23] They identified certain essential features for productive group work, one of which is that members should 'support each other in their joint efforts to complete the task and achieve the goal' through challenging others' reasoning, explaining their own ideas, responding to what others say and making constructive suggestions. The team say that the ability to work well in a group should not be assumed, as 'interpersonal and group skills need to be developed'; and they conclude that 'some negotiation of the ground rules for working together and occasional review of the process are important for successful interaction and cooperative learning'.

Ground rules can also help to overcome other inequalities. Sociolinguistic research confirms what many women have experienced: in mixed gender groups, male participants tend to dominate discussions. If the rules are clear, everyone can be expected to play by the same rules, whoever they are. In recordings when students are learning to use Exploratory Talk, I have heard female students remind others in the group to follow the ground rules. They can do so confidently because the whole class has signed up to this way of talking and working. By revealing and challenging the ways that mixed-gender discussions commonly unfold, oracy education can enable girls to become more confident speakers.[24] Making the ground rules explicit can also help to ensure the inclusion of autistic students, who often find it hard to infer the social norms that apply to a situation. Once the rules are made explicit, they have a much clearer idea of how to take part. As one autistic adult puts it: 'When there is a set way of doing things that everybody understands and adheres to, and we are all very clear on each other's roles and responsibilities, autistic people can fit neatly into the framework of a team.'[25]

Of course, cultural factors need to be considered when encouraging and enabling children (or adults) to use talk for thinking together. From working with researchers and teachers in Mexico, for example, I know that cultural expectations there make students less willing to be publicly critical about someone else's ideas than in the UK. Japanese researchers tell me that similar cultural norms apply in their country. In Israel and the Netherlands, though, it seems that directly criticising someone's ideas is not considered so rude, and can more easily be justified if it will help a group achieve a good outcome. This approach to developing collaborative oracy skills, suitably adapted to cultural norms, has been used successfully in such culturally diverse locations as Spain, Australia, Chile, Mexico, Norway, Iceland and China.[26] There are good reasons to believe it could improve the quality of collaborative activity in classrooms everywhere.

As well as improving group problem-solving, learning to use Exploratory Talk can have psychological benefits, and not just for students. It enables people to see another person's point of view and encourages everyone to explain their own ideas. Some problems are intractable, and some points of view are truly irreconcilable, but finding the solution to any problem is helped by considering the range of ideas that are relevant. Exploratory Talk requires people to make their reasoning explicit, and to evaluate what they hear from others. By thinking aloud, they become more aware of their own thinking processes. They can 'hear themselves think'. Sometimes it is difficult to clarify thoughts until they are precipitated into speech, and the presence of attentive listeners who are offering supportive or challenging ideas helps this happen. This, then, is one interesting effect of oracy education: learning oracy skills helps to develop *metacognitive* skills.

Exploratory Talk also highlights *how* we can contribute to joint problem-solving, as we become better at monitoring and planning our own intellectual activity. We think more reflectively and become more adept at *self-regulation*. The Education Endowment Foundation has concluded that the development of self-regulation and metacognition can have a profound impact on students' attainment in school; in some instances, researchers have recorded up to seven months' additional progress for students who learned the relevant skills.[27]

Through engaging in open dialogue with others in a supportive setting, we can develop another distinctive and important human capability – '*theory of mind*'. Exploratory Talk is a kind of dialogue that encourages us to apply our theory of mind; it enables us to become better at understanding one another. Through talking with others, we become more able to imagine the way the world looks from someone else's perspective; we start to build a theory of what is in their minds. This important human attribute is closely related to our uniquely social intelligence. We can create our own explanations for the ways people think and why they act as they do; we can make predictions about what they might do, based on our theory of their mind. Of course there are pitfalls to this. People's minds are a bit like the ocean: fluid, always changing, in the sway of currents and weather, varying between calm and storm. But getting to know someone as a friend, a colleague or as a family member, through talk, can help us to discern what and how they think.

There is an additional powerful psychological benefit of learning how to take part in Exploratory Talk, which relates to the work of the psychologist Vygotsky. If young children engage in reasoned dialogue with others, as listeners and contributors, then joint, collective thinking – interthinking – provides a model for the development of their own individual thinking. That is, Exploratory Talk helps them develop a rational approach to addressing problems and making sense of experience. We know that this link between oracy development and cognitive development exists from the results of a substantial programme of research involving universities and schools in the UK and Mexico called 'Thinking Together'.[28] As part of that research, my colleagues and I compared the problem-solving success of primary school children in British and Mexican schools, who had been taught to use Exploratory Talk by their teachers, with children in other similar schools where classroom life had gone on as normal. We gave groups of students a non-verbal test of reasoning – the Raven's Progressive Matrices, which its manual says: 'is used to measure abstract reasoning and fluid intelligence'. The groups of students who had agreed to follow the relevant ground rules did significantly better at solving the test's puzzles than those who had not learned to use Exploratory Talk. But that was not all. We gave individual students a different version of the same test, for them to complete alone. Students who had been taught how to use Exploratory Talk, and had practised it in groups, gained higher *individual* scores on that test than a matched set of students who had not been introduced to the 'ground rules' approach. Oracy education had not only improved those young people's skills in communicating – it had also enhanced their cognitive abilities.[29] Developing rational thinking must surely be as important an educational goal as providing students with information.

Beyond the school gates, a team led by Anita Woolley of Carnegie Mellon University reviewed research on what they call 'collective intelligence' – the general ability of a group to carry out a variety of tasks.[30] They particularly wanted to know why some groups performed better than others – and if the collective intelligence of a group could be explained just by measuring the intelligence of its individual members. They gave adults, in groups of three or five, a variety of problem-solving tasks. They found that the success of the group was better predicted by features of the group as a whole and by how members worked together, than by the IQ of its individual members. The groups with members who participated more equally were better at solving tasks than the groups in which one or two people dominated. In other words, everyone contributing to the joint task made those groups more 'intelligent'.

My colleagues and I have found that teachers working together to evaluate and plan lessons do so most successfully when they use Exploratory Talk.[31] That kind of discussion also helps musicians to rehearse together and creative teams to produce the best results.[32] By drawing most productively on the mental abilities of everyone who is collaborating, Exploratory Talk enables people to achieve more together than they ever could as individuals.

7. Teaching and Learning Through Talk

In 2011, the British charity the Communication Trust came up with a brilliant idea: No Pens Day Wednesday. On a designated day, participating schools organise a programme in which every activity is to be carried out without any students or teachers reading or writing. There has since been quite an enthusiastic take up of their campaign. Their original purpose was to focus attention on the educational needs of children who struggle to talk, but reports from schools suggest it has also had other benefits. As a senior manager of primary schools wrote in the *Guardian*: 'It was a great opportunity to go into a subject in more depth, without the constraint of writing, and gave us the chance to extend and explore vocabulary at a greater pace. Interestingly, some of the pupils who would not otherwise shine took the opportunity to really show us what they could do. The pupils loved the day. Many of them asked if we could hold No Pens Day Wednesday the next day too.'[1]

At school, I often found A-level biology lessons enthralling, while chemistry was one of the few times I have ever been able to sleep during the day. It was only later that I concluded that it was something to do with how the two teachers talked with us. In lessons, both spoke at length about their subject. Both sometimes asked us questions about the subject matter, but the chemistry teacher asked very few and just expected the right answer. The biology teacher, on the other hand, asked broader, more open questions and urged us to justify our answers. He was still rather abruptly critical of 'wrong' answers, but we certainly were encouraged to speak more than in chemistry. During my first year at university, I attended a reunion at which I told the biology teacher that his brilliant teaching had given me a head start in both physiology and philosophy of science. Rather than seeming pleased, he pointed at the headmaster and said: 'Tell that b—d over there!' His 'noisy' lessons had not been popular with senior staff. Even today, such attitudes remain common.

Managing talk is necessary when overseeing rooms of energetic young people. But if the purpose of school is education, rather than simply control, students' voices do not need to be supressed, but only marshalled in productive ways. That is why teachers need to be very aware of how they use talk themselves.

In 2024, Jonathan Noakes, the director of teaching at Eton College, was asked by the *Guardian* if state schools should set up more debating clubs. He thought they should, but I found what he said about talk in the classroom more revealing: 'We teach through discussion. It is not OK for a boy at Eton not to speak in lessons – and that makes a big difference. We also specifically train teachers to run lessons as discussions. In a teacher's first year at the school, we run coaching days for them throughout the year, and one of those looks at how best to generate discussions in class.'[2] I think it is important that he was talking about lessons generally, across the curriculum, and not just in English or other arts subjects. Many teachers we have worked with in state-funded schools would agree with him, though their views are less often sought.

In 2014, Christine Howe, Sara Hennessy and I successfully applied for funding from the Economic and Social Research Council to carry out one of the largest ever studies of talk and learning in primary classrooms. Small-scale, qualitative studies have prevailed in educational research, but while they provide very interesting and useful findings, their lack of scale has led to unfavourable comparisons with medical research, in which large amounts of data are typically gathered, analysed and subjected to rigorous statistical analysis.[3] Building on the findings of many smaller studies, we therefore designed a 'big data' project to discover how the best teachers used and organised talk.[4] We asked teachers of Year 6 students (aged 10–11) to let us observe and video them carrying out English and maths lessons as normal. Seventy-two teachers in forty-eight state schools in seven different counties of England participated. We did not make any suggestions about how or what they should teach.

In our analysis, we focused on two lessons carried out by each teacher, in which two different subjects were taught. This meant that we gave ourselves the very daunting task of analysing, in detail, more than 140 hours of talk by teachers and students. To assess the impact on students' learning, we used the results of statutory tests which all children in English primary schools take in their final year. These were the Standardised Assessment Tests, known as SATs.* I am no great fan of SATs, not least because of the strain they place on both teachers and students, but their attraction for our project was that they offered a completely independent assessment of achievement that would provide the kind of evidence that teachers, school managers and policymakers would respect. We also gathered information about other factors which might affect students' attainment, such as the social mix in a class, the proportion of those with English as a second language and the number of students with special needs.

* We also observed teachers carrying out science lessons; however, the science SATs were withdrawn by the government as we began the study. That meant we could not use SATs results to assess learning outcomes as we did for maths and English.

We completed this research by 2018. We found that Year 6 students improved significantly more in numeracy and literacy when:

1. Teachers achieved *high levels of participation* by their students in classroom dialogue. Studies of classroom interaction have noted that teachers usually direct questions at two kinds of students: those who can be relied upon to provide a sensible answer; and those who need to be reminded to pay attention. In contrast, the most successful teachers in our project managed to get many children to contribute to whole-class discussions, so that they were taking an active role.
2. Teachers got students to *elaborate* their ideas – to explain what they meant in more detail. For example, if a student said something which was interesting, or cryptic, the teacher might say: 'Can you explain a bit more what you mean by that?'
3. Teachers got students to *question* ideas and engage with what someone else said. For example, if one student offered an answer, they might ask another student: 'What do you think of Sanjay's suggestion?' or 'Do you agree or disagree with what Tom said? Why?'

Our conclusions aligned with many previous studies, but one of our findings was unique. It was that those three features only contributed to students' higher attainment if *all* of them happened. If a teacher involved lots of students in discussions, but never asked them to elaborate their ideas, it didn't work. Neither did only asking a few students, rather than many members of the class, to elaborate. And even if many students participated, if there was no critical engagement within discussions, there were no significant benefits for learning. Additionally, students in classes where the elaboration of ideas was encouraged had the most positive attitudes towards school.

I should make it clear that I do not think that all teachers need to do to get good results from contented students is to employ these three features of classroom talk. It is rather that I believe that when they occur frequently, those features indicate that a certain kind of oracy climate exists in a classroom, and that teachers are pursuing 'dialogic teaching'.[5]

Here is an example from one of the classes we observed, who had been studying the Antarctic expedition led by Ernest Shackleton in 1907. The children had been rather horrified to learn that, when food became short, Shackleton had ordered all the expedition's sled dogs to be shot. Their teacher drew on this interest by leading a discussion of the statement, 'It was right for the dogs to be shot.' This is a short extract from the much longer, lively dialogue:[6]

Saleem: Me and Mahir agreed that it was right, and we agreed and also disagreed with the statement, because they could have used the dogs for guard dogs or something like transportation.

Teacher: OK, OK, thank you for your point. Who would like to add or build on what Saleem's just said?

Malika: Building on what Saleem's said, I disagree because they have guard dogs (*long pause*). Say for example some of the men they were hunting and polar bears came, then guard dogs wouldn't be enough to guard their belongings.

Teacher: Who would like to build on from what Malika's just said?

Ayesha: I agree with Malika. The main priority was that it was right for them to shoot. If they hadn't shot the dogs, the dogs will die of starvation and that's more painful than dying of a shot because, if you die of a shot, it's only painful for like one second.

You can see that the children *elaborate* their ideas and justify them. They also *question* the views others put forward and explain why they agree or disagree. Notice too their uses of 'if', 'because' and other reasoning words like 'then'. Although this is a teacher-led discussion, it has some strong resemblances to Exploratory Talk.[7] We also observed groupwork and evaluated it in terms of the criteria for effective collaboration in Chapter 6 – essentially, whether students were using the right 'ground rules'. We found that when students collaborated well, this was also linked to better learning outcomes. Again, this supports the view that any teachers who avoid group work, or – just as limiting – do not teach their students how to do it well, are missing an important chance to improve both their students' oracy skills and their academic results.

You may also have noticed that some of the students' contributions were not 'grammatically correct'. Schools in which students are sanctioned if they reply to a teacher's question with anything other than a 'full sentence' or include any long pauses, 'umms' or 'aahs', make me despair. When people are speaking spontaneously, they rarely speak in full sentences. That is only natural since speakers are 'thinking on their feet', concentrating more on the content of what they say than its structure. In responding to teachers' questions, students are using talk to learn. If they have to worry about hesitating, they will not be concentrating on the relevant knowledge, but how they present it. If they were using talk for performance, such as giving a prepared speech, then of course different expectations would apply.

To put this in a broader context, here is an extract from a very different kind of educational setting: a class for young adults in London who are learning English as a second language.[8] The teacher asked each of the twenty students to describe themselves to the rest of the class:

Teacher: Who would like to tell the class about their personal qualities? Dalia?

Dalia: (*Reads from her notes.*) I am polite, friendly, organised, trustworthy, responsible but sometimes I am impatient and unpunctual. Sometimes (*laughs*).

Teacher: (*To the whole class.*) Good, isn't it? Thank you, Dalia. That was good. Now can you tell me the positive qualities you have just said.

Dalia: Yeah?

Teacher: That is, friendly, um, organised.

Dalia: Right.

Teacher: How is it helping you . . . with your friends in the class?

Dalia: It help me to get along with people and to understand them and help them.

Teacher: That's good. And what about the, the not very positive ones like unpunctual?

Dalia: Sometimes . . .

Teacher: What happens then?

Dalia: Sometimes I lose my friend basically of that because I lose my temper very quickly.

Teacher: And what happens with me? I don't smile at you that much, do I?

The teacher here was encouraging her student to elaborate her ideas. But she was not aiming for Dalia to develop her understanding of 'personal qualities'. Rather, she wanted to improve her student's confidence in speaking English in public. At a later date it might be appropriate for the teacher to correct Dalia's grammar, but at this point she was more concerned with helping her student to use English to think aloud.

Returning to the Cambridge project: such 'big data' studies of classroom talk are still rare. Its scale has only been matched by one that ran almost in parallel, involving teachers in seventy-six primary schools in the North and Midlands of England. That was the Dialogic Teaching Project, funded by the Education Endowment Foundation and carried out by a team led by Robin Alexander at the University of York.[9] They provided a cohort of Year 5 teachers with a form of oracy education by training them in dialogic teaching. Essentially, this meant getting them to interact with their classes in ways that previous research had suggested were most productive. So, for example, teachers began to use more 'open' questions in order to elicit extended and reasoned responses from their students. Then, using tests of English, maths and science specially designed for the purpose, the researchers compared the learning outcomes of students of those specially trained teachers with those from 'control group' schools. Statistical comparisons showed that the students of the 'dialogic' teachers achieved significantly better results in all three subjects. As the independent evaluation by Sheffield Hallam University put it: 'Children in Dialogic Teaching schools made two additional months' progress in English and science, and one additional month's progress in maths, compared to children in control schools, on average.'[10] The evaluators also reported that dialogic teaching was highly regarded by school heads and teachers, who said it had positive effects on students' confidence and engagement. The findings of the Cambridge and York projects are completely in accord. Together they provide strong support for a dialogic approach to classroom teaching.

How do the results of these two large projects relate to what some commentators, and a succession of Conservative ministers, have claimed is the essence of good teaching? Those advocates of a 'traditional' approach to education have argued that the prime role of the teacher is to deliver curriculum knowledge and that effective teaching means providing clear information and relevant instructions to silent, attentive classes, checking understanding by seeking 'right answers' to closed questions, and giving brief feedback on the answers elicited. From that perspective, any extended whole-class dialogue or group-based activity will only be a distraction. Clearly, the classroom-based evidence from the two projects I have described does not support that point of view. But I think such critics of dialogic teaching commonly misunderstand what it involves. Taking up a dialogic approach does not require a teacher to stop providing direct instruction to their students. The traditionalists are right to emphasise that teachers are experts with relevant knowledge and understanding of any subject, which they must impart to the novices in their classes. The role of the teacher in providing new information and explanations is crucial. But active participation in dialogue helps learners to make sense of new information, to make use of new vocabulary, to appreciate what they do or do not know, and to develop a deeper understanding of subject matter. Discussions among students, and between students and their teachers, can promote attainment in ways which the passive reception of information cannot. What is more, through dialogue with students, a teacher is more likely to gain insights into any misunderstandings or misconceptions that may have arisen than if students are simply asked to provide correct answers to closed questions.

Dialogic teaching does not correspond to the characteristics of some 'progressive' educational approaches either, which argue that a teacher's role should not be to 'deliver the curriculum' but to support students' self-directed learning. However, as in some 'progressive' classrooms, dialogic teaching gives students greater agency in their own learning than in the most 'traditional' settings. They are active participants in the creation of knowledge. In both the Cambridge and York projects, the teachers were following the prescribed content of the National Curriculum, and it was on their students' achievements in those subjects that they were judged. The students were not choosing their own learning paths or just following their inclinations. They were not being encouraged to 'chat'. But they were expected and enabled to take part in reasoned, productive discussions. And they were expected not just to retain and reproduce information, but collectively to make sense of it. Dialogic teaching does not require teachers to choose between being 'the sage on the stage' or 'the guide on the side'. As with most important things in life, being a good teacher cannot be reduced to such a simplistic choice.

Skilful teachers help students to understand a subject by doing more than simply telling them facts and expecting them to memorise them. The most successful teachers achieve a strategic balance between direct instruction, interactive dialogue and group-based activity. In case this all sounds rather abstract, let me give you another scenario from a real classroom. As part of a project on science teaching, my colleagues and I videoed sets of three consecutive Year 5 lessons on the solar system by the same teacher. In the first lesson, the teacher described the way the moon moves round the earth. In the second, she put the students into groups of three and gave them some 'Talking Point' statements to discuss and decide whether they were true or false. We have found that statements like these provoke discussions much more effectively than questions. Students tend to assume that any question has just one 'right answer'.[11] One of the statements was: 'The moon changes shape because it is in the shadow of the earth'. From the discussions that took place, like the one below, it was apparent that some students had not understood why the moon seems to change shape:

Viola: OK, (*reads*) 'The moon changes shape because it is in the shadow of the earth.'

Frannie: No, that's not true because there's the clouds that's covering the moon.

Viola: No, it isn't . . . Yes . . .

Gabrielle: Yes

Viola: Because in the day we think, oh the moon's gone, it hasn't gone, it's just clouds that

Frannie: Have covered it.

(*And a little later.*)

Viola: So what do we think?

Gabrielle: I think it's false.

Frannie: False.

After several minutes of talk in groups, the teacher brought them back together for a whole-class discussion:

Teacher: Keighley, would you read out number nine for us?
Keighley: (*Reads*) 'The moon changes shape because it is in the shadow of the earth.'
Teacher: Right, now what does your group think about that?
Keighley: True.
Teacher: What, um, why do you think that?
Keighley: Hm, because it's when earth is dark then, hm, not quite sure but we think it was true.
Teacher: Right, people with hands up – (*to Keighley*) who would you want to contribute?
Keighley: Um, Sadie?
Sadie: I think it's false because when the sun moves round the earth, it shines on the moon which projects down to the earth.
Teacher: (*To Sadie*) That sounds good. Do you want to choose somebody?
Sadie: Matthew.
Matthew: Well, we weren't actually sure 'cos we were thinking if the actual moon changes which it never does – or if it is our point of view from earth which it puts us in the shadow.
Teacher: That's a good point isn't it, it doesn't actually change, it looks as if it changes shape to us, that's a really good point.

This discussion continued for a while. The teacher's questions were designed to provoke thoughtful responses from the students. She asked them to elaborate, and they had to exercise their oracy skills in expressing their ideas. By providing different answers, they were also in effect questioning the viewpoints of other students. Many members of the class participated in the discussion. The teacher didn't immediately judge what students said as right or wrong, as she wanted to hear what they all thought. Some students made quite long contributions and, overall, they talked more than the teacher.

After the lesson had ended, I asked the teacher how she thought it had gone. She was not sanguine about it. It was evident from what they said that many of them did not yet understand how and why the moon goes through different phases. Her new plan for the next lesson was to set up on a table a model of the sun, earth and moon, using an electric table lamp, a globe and a tennis ball. This is how it went:

Teacher: Right, look, if the sun's shining from here (*lines up lamp, globe and tennis ball*) there is nothing between the sun and the moon, so from here on earth what we can see is a big circle, a big full shiny moon. Right? That's a full moon; we can see the whole caboodle, if we're here on earth and the sun's over there. However, have a look now, what happens now. If I put the moon here (*holds tennis ball between lamp and globe*) . . . here's the sun; is there any light from the sun falling on this moon that we would be able to see from earth?

Students: No.

The teacher continued in this way till she had shown how each phase of the moon happened. If students tried to speak then they were asked to wait, watch and listen. We move on now to the very end of this demonstration, which also coincided with the end of the lesson:

Teacher: And from earth we can only see about half of it, while the other half of it is this side. And this is how it works (*moves the moon round the earth*): dark, half-moon, full moon, half-moon, and that's what happens. With those little crescents in between. Viola? (*Viola has her hand up.*)

Viola: I've learned something now.

Teacher: Yes (*laughs*). I'm a bit worried about what. Go on then.

Viola: I didn't know that, I know that you can't see the other half, but I don't know how to explain it. (*Laughs*)

Teacher: Maybe you need to give it a chance for it to sink in and think about it; it's quite hard to understand; I find it hard to understand.

The lessons by this teacher were a good demonstration of dialogic teaching in practice.[12] What she learned from them through dialogue, rather than direct instruction, helped her plan some more effective instruction in the future – to which the students were now responsive. At the end of Year 6, her students got very good grades in science SATS.

There has been a lot of useful worldwide research on classroom talk. But so far, large-scale studies have only focused on talk in primary school classrooms, and only involved schools in England. We need similar 'big data' research involving students of different ages and in other countries. As with any aspects of oracy, the cultural contexts of classroom talk need to be considered. But teachers in all classrooms can teach *dialogically.* The success of classroom education everywhere depends on developing and applying the oracy skills of both teachers and students.

8. Into the Future

Talking is no trivial pursuit: oracy can be transformative – for individuals, groups, organisations and societies. Speaking and listening is vital for cognitive development, and enables us to share our individual experiences. By being taught how to think constructively with others, we can learn to think more critically on our own. Through using our voices to harness our social intelligence, our ability to interthink, we can find the solutions to life's burning questions. But we each have to learn how to do this well – and we cannot do so alone. Right from our earliest moments, we depend on other people to help us become effective communicators. That is why more attention needs to be given, at every level, to ensuring that all young children benefit from a rich experience of spoken language. Becoming a skilled speaker does not require sacrificing any slang or dialect, in favour of a more prestigious form; but it will involve learning new ways of communicating. The aim of educational policy and practice should be to broaden everyone's language repertoires, not to diminish them.

Careful research has shown that young people's academic achievement, and their attitudes to education, can be enhanced by productively using talk in classrooms – in the teaching of all subjects. Rather than taking a 'traditional' or 'progressive' approach, the most effective teaching is dialogic, which requires teachers themselves to be adept at oracy. Students need to engage actively with their teachers in the joint creation of knowledge, but they also need to become skilled at collaborating with others. 'Learning *how to* talk', 'Learning *about* talk' and 'Learning *through* talk' can enable young people to understand how spoken language works in social settings. Oracy education will prepare them for diverse occupations. It will also empower them to question the unspoken 'ground rules' that may prevent some voices from being heard.

The world of the next generation will not be the one we live in now. Oracy education will need to keep pace with evolving developments. There will be unexpected demands and opportunities for communication, especially through technology. Back in the nineteenth century, technology's impact on oracy was first felt through the arrival of the telephone. People celebrated being able to converse at a distance. But the use of phones led to the negotiation of novel forms of etiquette: how to introduce oneself, take turns and begin and end conversations. One obvious limitation was that callers had to comprehend what they heard without the visual clues that would normally be available in most face-to-face encounters. On the other hand, conversationalists gained the benefits of privacy. For example, a colleague once told me that, because she mistook the time, she had to take a telephone interview while out on a bike ride. (She got the job.)

In the twentieth century, other technological developments, such as broadcast media, created a demand for the different oracy skills involved in interviewing, reading the news, chairing discussions, presenting shows, commentating on sport and forecasting the weather. It is not surprising that, in the UK at least, such occupations have been disproportionally held by former students of private schools, which typically have always provided some oracy education.

Technology has now made it easy for us to both hear and see each other when we converse at a distance. This became a common feature of everyday life during the 2020–21 pandemic, during online family meetups and games sessions. And, of course, it enabled joint work practices to continue when travel was forbidden. For most of us, this required a rapid induction into ways of interacting in the virtual world. There are some clear advantages to talking online compared with meetings held in the same room. You can connect with people in different time zones and thousands of miles apart – without having to book flights or get stuck in a traffic jam. Discussions can be recorded and rewatched so that people can catch up on what they missed. But there are some disadvantages, too. You cannot easily make an 'aside' comment to the person next to you. The technology is still unreliable. And in my experience, misunderstandings arise more often online, and are more likely to be left unresolved, without the opportunities for clarification which would be possible by, say, going for a coffee once a meeting had ended. After face-to-face meetings, informal discussions naturally occur and some useful off-the-record things may be said.[1]

As with the telephone, new ground rules have been invented as we go along for online discussions. When or when not to 'mute'? Is it acceptable to attend a meeting but keep your screen turned off throughout? Is it OK for pets or children to appear on camera?

Virtual meetings and lectures are now the 'new normal'. The skills with which teachers generate and manage them are just as important on online platforms as in conventional classrooms. One young member of my family has experienced most of her secondary school education online, including group work with other students. It is a tribute to her teachers that she speaks well of it.

A very different technological impact on oracy has arisen through artificial intelligence. Because of concerns about students' use of AI tools when writing their essays, there has been a renewed interest in oral assessment. This may take the form of a question-and-answer session, a presentation or the kind of formal conversation known as a viva voce examination. Of course, this makes distinctive oracy demands on students. They need to learn how to do themselves justice in such a situation – to appreciate what speech register is appropriate, to make judgements about saying too much, or too little. My colleagues and I have worked with the Open University to help their students to prepare for such demands.

While I was writing this book, I decided to ask a chatbot, Google's Gemini, about oracy. It wrote back:

> 'Oracy is definitely important today! In a world that's increasingly connected, being able to express yourself clearly and confidently is a valuable skill.'[2]

We also now talk with chatbots. In my experience, AI 'agents' can be surprisingly realistic.[3] Their realism is achieved through machine learning: a kind of autodidactic oracy education. By sampling an enormous database of conversations, a chatbot becomes increasingly able to interact convincingly. Some AI services even offer to teach us oracy skills, claiming that they can help us prepare for talk events like interviews, or become better conversationalists.[4]

My colleague Paul Warwick was a member of a University of Cambridge/University of Oslo team that created

Talkwall, a microblogging tool which enables groups of students working collaboratively in different classrooms to share and discuss their ideas.[5] He has a special interest in the relationship between oracy and AI, and explains that 'The issue is the same for everyone, I think – the casual user, professionals, students of all ages; knowing what you want from an interaction with AI is one thing, knowing how to get the best out of the interaction is another . . . The key thing is that it's about how to have a productive dialogue. Beyond that, I'm beginning to hear that children are forming relationships with AI on platforms like ChatGPT, playing games with it, having conversations, etc – an imaginary friend that isn't imaginary.'

Skilled AI conversationalists are just our avatars; the ability to use language remains quintessentially human. Although literacy rates continue to increase, for most people in the world today spoken language is still their primary mode of communication. There is no doubt that spoken language skills will continue to be essential in many occupations and for active civic engagement. Education should enable citizens of the future to become self-confident communicators. That will help them to exercise more control over their own lives and make more contributions to their communities.

It may seem that I am claiming that oracy is naturally a force for good: that if we all learn to engage empathetically and effectively, the world will inevitably become a better place. I am not. Like literacy and numeracy, oracy is a toolkit without inbuilt ethical values. The oratory skills of Adolf Hitler helped to launch World War II; terrorist groups and criminal gangs may improve their tactics through reasoned discussion. But dialogue can reconcile different points of view and achieve settlements in ways that continuing violence never can. Oracy skills enable mediators in key international organisations to negotiate.[6] Words can change the future.

Whatever lies ahead, we will still need to talk. In fact, the ability to communicate well has never been needed more urgently. As I write, the world itself is in peril from wars, extreme political divisions, a heating planet and the destruction of the natural environment. Our unique language skills have helped to make us the dominant species on the planet, but we need to use them now to tackle the challenges we face. That is why oracy should no longer be the poor relation of literacy and numeracy. It should have pride of place in education systems, worldwide.

Oracy education cannot, in itself, break down social inequalities or barriers to opportunity. But it can play a vital role in confronting such barriers and challenging them as unjust. It can expose prejudice and discrimination. It can promote the status of the endangered languages and cultures of marginalised communities. It can enable a person, or a group of people, to pursue their goals; and it can be used to challenge rhetorics of power, to question whether what is said is true or false. By ensuring that it is not just the voices of the most assertive, wealthy and privileged that define our world, the pursuit of oracy enables us all to build a more inclusive, fairer society.

Notes

Introduction

1 Wilkinson, A. (1965). *Spoken English*. Birmingham: Birmingham University Press.
2 https://voice21.org/ (accessed 6.12.24)
3 *We need to talk: The report of The Commission of the Future of Oracy in England.* https://oracyeducationcommission.co.uk/ (accessed 20.11.24)
4 4 School 21 was founded by Peter Hyman, Ed Fidoe and Oli de Boton. See https://school21.org.uk/head-heart-and-hand/ (accessed 17.01.25)
5 'Keir Starmer unveils Labour's mission to break down barriers to opportunity at every stage', 6 July 2023. https://labour.org.uk/updates/press-releases/keir-starmer-unveils-labours-mission-to-break-down-barriers-to-opportunity-at-every-stage/ (accessed 24.11.24)
6 Clarkson, J. (2023). 'Starmer's talking out of his oracy. Teach kids to change a tyre', *The Times*, 9 July 2023. https://www.thetimes.com/uk/politics/article/jeremy-clarkson-starmers-talking-out-of-his-oracy-teach-kids-to-change-a-tyre-zvbq7zqob (accessed 25.11.24)

7 Cameron, D. (2025). *The Trouble with Oracy?*, Chapter 14 of T. Wright (ed.), *Oracy: The politics of speech education*. Cambridge: Cambridge University Press.

8 Wright, T. (2025). 'What the Chartists and Suffragettes Realised About Oracy', Chapter 11 of T. Wright (ed.), *Oracy: The politics of speech education*. Cambridge: Cambridge University Press.

9 In the UK, for example, Talk the Talk: https://talkthetalkuk.org; Debatemate: https://debatemate.com; and Debating for Everyone: www.debatingforeveryone.com (accessed 3.12.24)

1. Talking Ourselves Up

1 Pinker, S. (1994). *The Language Instinct*. London: Penguin, p. 15.

2 Dunbar, R. (1998). 'The social brain hypothesis'. *Evolutionary Anthropology*, 6, 178–189.

3 Tager-Flusberg, H. (2007). 'Evaluating the Theory-of-Mind Hypothesis of Autism'. *Current Directions in Psychological Science*, 16 (6), 311–315. https://doi.org/10.1111/j.1467-8721.2007.00527.x

4 Critchlow, H. (2022). *Joined-Up Thinking*. London: Hodder & Stoughton, p. 193.

5 Bakhtin, M. (1981). *The Dialogic Imagination*. Austin: University of Texas Press. He actually wrote: 'the word does

not exist in a neutral and impersonal language (it is not, after all, out of a dictionary that the speaker gets his words!), but rather it exists in other people's mouths'.

2. *An Early Start to Oracy*

1 'Adorable Baby with Scouse Accent Refusing Bedtime Routine', *Liverpool Echo*. https://www.tiktok.com/@liverpoolecho/video/7383692533341228321?lang=en (accessed 20.11.24)

2 Michael Rosen in the introduction to *Every Child a Talker: Guidance for early language lead practitioners* (2008). Department for Children, Schools and Families. Available at: https://resources.leicestershire.gov.uk/sites/resource/files/field/pdf/2017/1/16/ecat_first_instalment.pdf

3 Masek, L. R., McMillan, B. T., Paterson, S. J., Tamis-LeMonda, C. S., Michnick Golinkoff, M., Hirsh-Pasek, K. (2021). 'Where language meets attention: How contingent interactions promote learning'. *Developmental Review*, 60, 100961.

4 On her website, my colleague Topsy Page describes some good strategies for starting up dialogues with children: https://www.topsypage.com. There are also some lively ideas for getting children talking in Kavin Wadhar's excellent book *Little Big Conversations*: https://www.kidcoach.app/book. And you will find other useful

strategies for developing conversations with young children in Wendy Lee's *Oracy Cambridge blog*: https://oracycambridge.org/communicating-with-children/ (accessed 25.11.24)

5 Reese, E., Haden, C. A. & Fivush, R. (1993). 'Mother-child conversations about the past: Relationships of style and memory over time'. *Cognitive Development*, 8, 403–430.

6 Tõugu, P., Tulviste, T., Schröder, L. (2023). 'Making sense of the pandemic: Parent-child conversations in two cultural contexts', *PLOS ONE* 18(1): e0280781. https://doi.org/10.1371/journal. pone.0280781 (accessed 20.11.24)

7 See Chapter 3 of Gera, D. L. (2003). *Ancient Greek Ideas on Speech, Language and Civilization*. Oxford: Oxford University Press.

8 This is apparent in UK education policy statements such as the 1921 Newbolt Report: *The Teaching of English in England (being the Report of the Departmental Committee Appointed by the President of the Board of Education to Inquire into the Position of English in the Educational System of England)*. http://www.educationengland.org.uk/documents/newbolt/newbolt1921.html (accessed 20.11.24)

9 Hart, B. & Risley, T. R. (1995). *Meaningful Differences in the Everyday Experience of Young American Children*. New York: Brookes.

10 See, for example, Michaels, S. (2013). 'Commentary: Déjà Vu All Over Again: What's Wrong With Hart & Risley and a "Linguistic Deficit" Framework in Early Childhood

Education?', *LEARNing Landscapes*. 7. 23–41. 10.36510/learnland.v7i1.627.

11 The classic early study of such differences was: Brice Heath, S. (1982). *Ways with Words: Language, life, and work in communities and classrooms*, New York and Cambridge: Cambridge University Press.

12 Sperry, D. E., Sperry, L. L. & Miller, P. J. (2019). 'Re-examining the Verbal Environments of Children From Different Socioeconomic Backgrounds', *Child Development*, 90 (4):1303–1318. DOI: 10.1111/cdev.13072. Epub 2018 Apr 30. PMID: 29707767.

13 Roy, P., Chiat, S. & Dodd, B. (2014). *Language and Socioeconomic Disadvantage: From research to practice*. London, UK: City University London.

14 'Building Children's Vocabulary at Home & School: The Oxford Language Report 2023–2024'. https://global.oup.com/education/press/oxford-language-report-2023-4-in-10-pupils-have-fallen-behind/?region=uk (accessed 20.11.24); see also 'Bridging the Word Gap at Transition: The Oxford Language Report 2020', Oxford University Press with the Centre for Education and Youth. https://cfey.org/wp-content/uploads/2020/10/Bridging-the-Word-Gap-at-Transition-2020-Menzies-et-al-2020.pdf (accessed 20.11.24)

15 Kartushina, N. et al. (2022). 'COVID-19 first lockdown as a unique window into language acquisition: What you do (with your child) matters', *Language Development Research*, 2, 1.

https://www.mpi.nl/publications/item3292449/covid-19-first-lockdown-window-language-acquisition-associations-between (accessed 14.4.24)

16 Britton, J. (1970). *Language and Learning*. Harmondsworth: Penguin.

17 The NELI programme: https://www.teachneli.org/ (accessed 30.11.24)

18 'National roll-out of Covid recovery programme boosted young children's language skills by four months', EEF. https://educationendowmentfoundation.org.uk/news/national-roll-out-of-covid-recovery-programme-boosted-young-childrens-language-skills-by-four-months (accessed 30.11.24)

19 Vygotsky, L. S. (1962). *Thought and Language*. Cambridge, Mass.: MIT Press. For a discussion of the educational importance of Vygotsky's work, see Daniels, H. (2001). *Vygotsky and Pedagogy*. London, UK: Routledge/ Falmer.

20 Cole, M. (2009). 'The Perils of Translation: A First Step in Reconsidering Vygotsky's Theory of Development in Relation to Formal Education', *Mind, Culture and Activity*, 16(4):291–295.

21 Tantucci, V. (2024). 'How patterns of conversation could help identify early signs of autism in children', *The Conversation*, 9 September. https://theconversation.com/how-patterns-of-conversation-could-help-identify-early-signs-of-autism-in-children-227499 (accessed 1.12.24)

22 'Developmental Language Disorder (DLD)', *Speech and Language UK*. https://speechandlanguage.org.uk/educators-and-professionals/resource-library-for-educators/developmental-language-disorder-dld/ (accessed 24.11.24)

23 'Lily Farrington's Amazing Developmental Language Disorder Animation'. https://www.youtube.com/watch?v=rwOfkjodj_o (accessed 30.11.24)

24 'Listening to unheard children: a shocking rise in speech and language challenges', *Speech and Language UK*. https://speechandlanguage.org.uk/the-issue/our-campaigns/listening-to-unheard-children/ (accessed 20.11.24)

25 See, for example, the 'What works' website of Speech and Language UK: https://speechandlanguage.org.uk/educators-and-professionals/what-works-database/register/. Also see the website of my Oracy Cambridge colleague Wendy Lee, a speech therapist, who provides links to a wealth of useful resources: https://www.lingospeech.co.uk

26 Bialystok, E. & Feng, X. (2010). 'Language proficiency and its implications for monolingual and bilingual children', in A. Durgunoglu & Goldenberg, C. (eds.) (2011). *Dual Language Learners: The development and assessment of oral and written language*. New York: Guilford Press. pp. 121–138.

27 Xia, T., An, Y. and Guo, J. (2022). 'Bilingualism and Creativity: Benefits from cognitive inhibition and cognitive flexibility', *Frontiers in Psychology*, 13:1016777.

28 For a general discussion of bilingualism see Grosjean, F. (2010). *Bilingual: Life and reality*. Cambridge, Mass: Harvard University Press.

3. The Oracy Skills Framework

1 Stokoe, E. (2018). *Talk: The science of conversation*. Robinson: London.

2 Voice 21 provide good justifications for assessing oracy skills. https://voice21.org/oracy-can-be-assessed/. See also https://rethinkingassessment.com/rethinking-blogs/assessing-the-impact-of-oracy-on-your-students/ (accessed 24.11.24)

3 The Programme for International Student Assessment (PISA) has trialled the assessment of speaking and listening, but focused on young people's foreign language use. https://www.oecd.org/en/topics/sub-issues/foreign-language-learning/pisa-2025-foreign-language-assessment.html

4 Assessment of Performance Unit (APU) (1988). *Language performance in schools: Review of APU language monitoring 1979–1983*. London: Her Majesty's Stationary Office, p. 64.

5 QCDA (2010). 'Understanding English, communication and languages'. https://www.google.com/url?sa=t&source=web&rct=j&opi=89978449&url=https://dera.ioe.ac.uk/id/eprint/10540/8/QCDA-Understanding_

English-AoL.doc&ved=2ahUKEwjPpp3dtuuJAxUqUUEAHfULGo8QFnoECBQQAQ&usg=AOvVaw13mIY9bYypWUQrQnsumoNR (accessed 20.11.24)

6 Ofqual (2013). 'Analysis of responses to the consultation on the proposal to remove speaking and listening assessment from the GCSE English and GCSE English language grade', Ofqual Report number 13/5317. https://dera.ioe.ac.uk/id/eprint/17586/7/2013-08-29-analysis-of-responses-to-the-consultation-removal-of-speaking-and-listening.pdf (accessed 07.01.24)

7 'The Scottish survey of literacy and numeracy, 2016'. https://www.gov.scot/publications/scottish-survey-literacy-numeracy-2016-literacy/ (accessed 25.11.24)

8 'PISA 2015: Collaborative problem solving'. https://www.oecd.org/en/topics/sub-issues/student-problem-solving-skills/pisa-2015-collaborative-problem-solving.html

9 The website states: 'Students need to read, write, speak, listen, and use language effectively across a wide range of content areas, and these standards support the development of those skills in all disciplines.' https://www.thecorestandards.org/ELA-Literacy/ (accessed 6.12.24)

10 https://www.thecorestandards.org/ELA-Literacy/SL/8/

11 The Oracy Assessment Toolkit. https://www.educ.cam.ac.uk/research/programmes/oracytoolkit/ (accessed 25.11.24)

12 'Excelerate launches oracy training initiative', The Wood Foundation. https://www.thewoodfoundation.org.uk/excelerate-launches-oracy-training-initiative/ (accessed 20.11.24)
13 Alexander, R. (2020). *A Dialogic Teaching Companion*. Abingdon: Routledge, p. 77.
14 Gove, M. (2013). 'Michael Gove speaks about the importance of teaching'. https://www.gov.uk/government/speeches/michael-gove-speaks-about-the-importance-of-teaching (accessed 25.11.24)
15 Bridget Phillipson, quoted in 'Education for 11 to 16-year-olds: House of Lords committee report', *In Focus*, 23 July 2024. https://lordslibrary.parliament.uk/education-for-11-to-16-year-olds-house-of-lords-committee-report/ (accessed 20.11.24)
16 Colville, R. (2023). 'Sit down and pay attention! The evidence is clear – stricter schools get better results'. *Sunday Times*, 21 October 2023.
17 Michaela Community School. https://michaela.education (accessed 20.11.24)
18 'The Co-Curriculum', Eton College. https://www.etoncollege.com/outside-the-classroom/our-ethos/ (accessed 25.11.24)
19 Education Policy Institute. *Annual Report 2024: Social Mobility and Vulnerable Learners*. https://epi.org.uk/publications-and-research/annual-report-2024/ (accessed 21.11.24)

20 Coleman, S. (2025). *Releasing Civic Voices.* Chapter 13 of T. Wright, (ed.), *Oracy: The politics of speech education.* Cambridge: Cambridge University Press.

21 Mannion, James: 'The Transformative power of oracy'. *Oracy Cambridge blog*, February 2023. https://oracycambridge.org/oracy-at-the-heart-of-the-curriculum/

22 Perez-Adamson, C. & Mercer, N. (2015). 'How do different types of schools prepare students for life at Cambridge?', *Cambridge Journal of Education*, 46(1):1–17. DOI:10.1080/0305764X.2015.1009364.

23 'State school pupils do better at university, Cambridge Assessment research confirms', Cambridge Assessment (2015). https://www.cambridgeassessment.org.uk/news/state-school-pupils-do-better-at-university-cambridge-assessment-research-confirms/ (accessed 25.11.24)

24 There is a growing interest in the UK in the provision of oracy education for students in higher education. See Heron, M., Baker, S., Gravett, K. & Irwin, E. (2022). 'Scoping academic oracy in higher education: knotting together forgotten connections to equity and academic literacies', *Higher Education Research & Development*, 42(1), 62–77.

25 Lakoff, R. T. (2004). *Language and Woman's Place: Text and commentaries.* Oxford: Oxford University Press.

26 Baxter, J. A. (1999). 'Teaching Girls to Speak Out: The Female Voice in Public Contexts, *Language and Education*, 13 (2), pp. 81–98.

27 Wagner, C. (2023). '"Diminished Voices": Why is it important to focus on oracy when educating girls?' *Oracy Cambridge blog*, 7 June. https://oracycambridge.org/diminished-voices-girls-oracy/ (accessed 25.11.24)

4. Talking Proper

1 'We Need to Talk: The Report of The Commission of the Future of Oracy in England', see particularly Sections 4.43 and 4.44. https://oracyeducationcommission.co.uk/ (accessed 20.11.24)

2 The Buchan Heritage Society. http://buchanheritagesociety.co.uk/

3 https://www.scotsman.com/whats-on/arts-and-entertainment/billy-connolly-recalls-speech-impediment-anger-at-efforts-to-tone-down-accent-3357021 (accessed 24.11.24)

4 Alexandria, C. (2022). 'What is the Relationship Between Language, Race & Class in London?' https://blackfeministcollective.com/2022/05/13/black-british-english-what-is-the-relationship-between-language-race-class-in-london/ (accessed 20.11.24)

5 Drummond, R. (2016). 'Leave off, will you? Britain should celebrate "regional" accents', *The Conversation*. https://theconversation.com/leave-off-will-you-britain-should-celebrate-regional-accents-67952

6 Levon, E., Sharma, D. & Ilbury, C. (2002). 'Speaking up: accents and social mobility', The Sutton Trust. https://www.suttontrust.com/our-research/speaking-up-accents-social-mobility/ (accessed 24.11.24)

7 Giles, H., & Powesland, P. F. (1975). *Speech Style and Social Evaluation.* New York, NY: Academic Press.

8 Accent Bias Britain. https://accentbiasbritain.org (accessed 21.11.24)

9 Levon, E., Sharma, D., Watt, D. J., Cardoso, A., &Ye, Y. (2021). 'Accent Bias and Perceptions of Professional Competence in England', *Journal of English Linguistics*, 49(4) 355–388.

10 Drummond, R. (2023). *You're All Talk.* London: Scribe Publications.

11 His fellow Lancastrian, Cat Smith MP, has joked: 'It's good to have someone in the chair who doesn't have an accent'. https://x.com/CatSmithMP/status/1811300669602631699 (accessed 24.11.24)

12 Jess Phillips quoted in 'One in four have accents mocked at work – survey', BBC News, 3 November 2022. https://www.bbc.co.uk/news/uk-63494849 (accessed 1.12.24)

13 Heselwood, B., & McChrystal, L. (2000). 'Gender, accent features and voicing in Panjabi-English bilingual children', *Leeds Working Papers in Linguistics and Phonetics*, 8(1), 45–70. See also https://www.leedsbeckett.ac.uk/blogs/carnegie-education/2021/05/accent-identity-and-prejudice/

14 'Joan Bakewell: Why I dropped my northern accent'. https://www.bbc.co.uk/programmes/p045zmb8 (accessed 20.11.24)

15 Lucia Ritucci, 'Why do you talk so white?'.https://static1.squarespace.com/static/56de82321d07c0069b7ca515/t/5d0797710135 8a0001b55ada/1560778609940/Lucia+Ritucci_+Why+do+you+talk+so+white_.pdf (accessed 20.11.24)

16 See, for example, Paul Carley, 'Speak clearly to be taken seriously'. https://paulcarley.com. (accessed 20.11.24)

17 Sly, E. (1922). 'Why dialects are still important', *Italia Segreda*. https://italysegreta.com/why-italian-dialects-are-still-important/ (accessed 20.11.24)

18 BBC Bitesize: KS2 'Using standard and non-standard English'. https://www.bbc.co.uk/bitesize/articles/zp9jkty#zc3fcxs

19 CASITA: 'Master Roadman Slang'. https://www.casita.com/blog/master-roadman-slang (accessed 20.11.24)

20 Some linguists differentiate between 'code-switching' (changing languages) and 'style switching' (changing varieties or registers). See Chapter 4 of Drummond, R. (2023). *You're All Talk*. London: Scribe Publications.

21 De Meo, M. (2020). 'Subtitling dialect in *Inspector Montalbano* and *Young Montalbano*', *inTRAlinea*, Special Issue: *The Translation of Dialects in Multimedia IV*. https://www.intralinea.org/specials/article/2466 (accessed 20.11.24)

22 McCluney, C. L., Robotham, K., Lee, S., Smith, R. & Durkee, M. (2019). 'The costs of code-switching', *The Big Idea Series.* https://hbr.org/2019/11/the-costs-of-codeswitching
23 Wiltz, A. (2020). *How Code-Switching Causes More Harm Than Good.* https://aninjusticemag.com/how-code-switching-causes-more-harm-than-good-18ede1a57ba0 (accessed 24.11.24)
24 'Zephaniah speaks', *The Puffin Post,* 1997. https://benjaminzephaniah.com/the-puffin-post/?doing_wp_cron=1732110434.9379220008850097656250 (accessed 20.11.24)
25 Lanza, E. (2004). *Language Switching in Infant Bilingualism: A sociolinguistic perspective.* New York: Oxford University Press.
26 *Benjamin Zephaniah's Promotion of Multiple British Identities.* Posted by Zepheniagroup, 6 July 2017. https://britishidentitiessite.wordpress.com/2017/07/06/zephania-2-paragraphs/ (Accessed 20.11.24)
27 Shafiq, Q. (2025). 'Fluency for me, but not for thee: Why disadvantaged pupils deserve oracy', Chapter 3 of T. Wright (ed.), *Oracy: The Politics of Speech Education.* Cambridge: Cambridge University Press.
28 Cushing, I. & Snell, J. (2022). 'The (white) ears of Ofsted: A raciolinguistic perspective on the listening practices of the schools inspectorate'. *Language in Society,* 52. 1. doi:10.1017=S0047404522000094.
29 Cushing, I. (2025). 'Oracy and Social (In)Justice', Chapter 2 of T. Wright (ed.), *Oracy: The Politics of Speech Education.* Cambridge: Cambridge University Press.

30 I have taken this idea from Jay Lemke: Lemke, J. (1990). *Talking Science: Language, learning, and values*. Norwood, NJ: Ablex Publishing.

31 Sherrington, T. (2017). 'Empowering speech, challenges on 'correctness' and some questions for sociolinguists', *Teacherhead*. https://teacherhead.com/2017/10/26/empowering-speech-challenges-on-correctness-and-some-questions-for-sociolinguists/ (accessed 20.11.24)

5. Speaking in Public

1 'What do Britons say they have a phobia of?', YouGov, 27 Feb 2023. https://yougov.co.uk/society/articles/45297-what-do-britons-say-they-have-phobia. See also Grieve, R., Woodley, J., Hunt, S. & McKay, A. (2021). 'Student fears of oral presentations and public speaking in higher education: A qualitative survey', *Journal of Further and Higher Education*, DOI: 10.1080/0309877X.2021.1948509.

2 'Almost half of corporations highest paid stars went to private school, figures reveal', *Independent*, 22 July 2017. https://www.independent.co.uk/news/uk/home-news/bbc-pay-private-school-highest-paid-half-stars-salaries-breakdown-a7854491.html (accessed 21.11.24)

3 The University of Cambridge offers an online public speaking course: https://advanceonline.cam.ac.uk/courses/compelling-communication-skills/ (accessed 25.11.24)

4 The Oxford Union. https://oxford-union.org (accessed 21.11.24)

5 Angela Rayner, MP, 'About me'. https://www.angelarayner.co.uk/about/ (accessed 21.11.24)

6 Gaunt, A. & Stott, A. (2019). *Transform Teaching and Learning Through Talk: The oracy imperative*. London: Rowman & Littlefield.

7 Davies, S. (2019). 'Heard the one about the working-class comedian? It's no joke for us', *Guardian*, 10 September 2019.

8 As is well argued by Amy Gaunt and Alice Stott of Voice 21: Gaunt, A. & Stott, A. (2019). *Transform Teaching and Learning Through Talk: The oracy imperative*. London: Rowman & Littlefield.

9 Horak, E. (2023). 'The Fluency Myth of proper Communication', 8 August 2003. https://stamma.org/your-voice/fluency-myth-proper-communication (accessed 21.11.24)

10 Trevor Cox describes such techniques as imbuing a speaker with 'vocal charisma'. Cox, T. (2018). *Now You're Talking: Human conversation from the neanderthals to artificial intelligence*. London: Bodley Head.

11 School 21. https://school21.org.uk/oracy/ (accessed 21.11.24)

12 James Mannion, 'The Transformative power of oracy'. *Oracy Cambridge blog*, February 2023. https://oracycambridge.org/oracy-at-the-heart-of-the-curriculum

13 Voice 21: Impact Report 2022–2023. https://voice21.org/impact-report-2022-2023/ (accessed 24.11.24)
14 'Greta Thunberg's Speech At The U.N. Climate Action Summit', 23 Sept 2019. https://www.npr.org/2019/09/23/763452863/transcript-greta-thunbergs-speech-at-the-u-n-climate-action-summit
15 See Broome, T. (2024). 'US election: How Trump's speeches echo Roman rhetoric and style from 2,000 years ago', *The Conversation*, 16 August 2024. https://theconversation.com/us-election-how-trumps-speeches-echo-roman-rhetoric-and-style-from-2-000-years-ago-235618 (accessed 6.12.24)
16 Svehla, L., Lyons, W. (2024). 'The Audacity of Trump: The Rhetorical Strategy of President Donald Trump' in: Grossman, M., Schortgen, F., Matthews Jr., R. E., Cohen, D. B. (eds.), *The Legacy of the Trump Administration: The evolving American presidency*. Palgrave Macmillan, Cham. https://doi.org/10.1007/978-3-031-65247-9_9 (accessed 25.11.24)
17 Sclafani, J. (2017). *Talking Donald Trump: A sociolinguistic study of style, metadiscourse, and political identity*. London: Routledge, 2017.
18 Hughes, C. (2020). 'Thou Art in a Deal: The Evolution of Religious Language in the Public Communications of Donald Trump', *International Journal of Communication*, volume: 20, 4825–4846.
19 Savin, S. & Treisman, D. (2024). 'We analyzed 9 years of Trump political speeches, and his violent rhetoric has

increased dramatically'. *The Conversation*, 26 October 2024. https://theconversation.com/we-analyzed-9-years-of-trump-political-speeches-and-his-violent-rhetoric-has-increased-dramatically-238962 (accessed 25.11.24)

20 Viser, M. (2015). 'For presidential hopefuls, simpler language resonates', *The Boston Globe*, 20 October 2015. https://www.bostonglobe.com/news/politics/2015/10/20/donald-trump-and-ben-carson-speak-grade-school-level-that-today-voters-can-quickly-grasp/LUCBY6u-wQAxiLvvXbVTSUN/story.html (accessed 21.11.24)

21 Keir Starmer's speech on fixing the foundations of our country, 27 August 2024. https://www.gov.uk/government/speeches/keir-starmers-speech-on-fixing-the-foundations-of-our-country-27-august-2024 (accessed 21.11.24)

6. Collaboration

1 Maneesh Sahani, professor of theoretical neuroscience and machine learning at University College London, quoted in the *Guardian*, 11 October 2024. https://www.theguardian.com/science/2024/oct/11/nobel-awards-highlight-britains-ai-pedigree-demis-hassabis-geoffrey-hinton (accessed 24.11.24)

2 Mercer, A. (2019). *The Collaborative Literary Relationship of Percy Bysshe Shelley and Mary Wollstonecraft Shelley*. Abingdon: Routledge.

3 John-Steiner, V. (2000). *Creative Collaboration.* New York: Oxford University Press.

4 'Ten 21st-century skills every student needs', *World Economic Forum*, 10 March 2016. https://www.weforum.org/stories/2016/03/21st-century-skills-future-jobs-students/ (accessed 25.11.24)

5 *Employer Skills Survey, 2015*, UK Commission for Employment and Skills. https://assets.publishing.service.gov.uk/media/5ae8678d40f0b631578af072/Employer_Skills_Survey_2015_UK_Results-Amended-2018.pdf(accessed 21.11.24)

6 *PISA 2015 Collaborative Problem Solving.* Since 2015 the OECD has assessed young people's collaborative problem-solving by using a computer-based simulation. They found that girls performed better than boys on the test. Organisation for Economic Co-operation and Development (OECD). https://www.oecd.org/en/topics/sub-issues/student-problem-solving-skills/pisa-2015-collaborative-problem-solving.html

7 Glaser, J. E. (2014). *Conversational Intelligence.* Brookline, MA: Bibliomotion.

8 Janis, I. (1982). *Groupthink: Psychological studies of policy decisions and fiascoes*, 2nd edn, New York: Houghton Mifflin.

9 'Ever since the debate, Biden and his closest aides had been determined to rebound, convinced that he remained his party's best chance to defeat former President Donald

Trump and optimistic that they could contain the fallout.' 'Why Biden finally quit', *Politico*, 21 July 2024. https://www.politico.com/news/2024/07/21/why-biden-dropped-out-00170106 (accessed 21.11.24)

10 Jacobi, T., & Schweers, D. (2017). 'Justice, Interrupted: The Effect of Gender, Ideology and Seniority at Supreme Court Oral Arguments', *103 Virginia Law Review* 1379 (2017), Northwestern Law & Econ Research Paper No. 17-03. Available at SSRN: https://ssrn.com/abstract=2933016 (accessed 21.11.24)

11 Dhairyawan, R. (2024). *Unheard: The medical practice of silencing.* London: Hachette.

12 Tannen, D. (1984). *Conversational Style: Analysing talk amongst friends.* Norwood, NJ, Ablex.

13 Mercer, N. (2019) *Language and the Joint Creation of Knowledge: The selected works of Neil Mercer.* Abingdon: Routledge. Chapters 3, 7 and 9. See also Mercer, N. & Littleton, K. (2007). *Dialogue and the Development of Children's Thinking.* London: Routledge.

14 Barnes, D. (2008). 'Exploratory talk for learning', in N. Mercer & S. Hodgkinson (eds.), *Exploring talk in school: Inspired by the work of Douglas Barnes.* London: Sage. In the USA, such discussion is usually called 'Accountable Talk'. Resnick, L., Asterhan, C. & Clarke, S. (2018). *Accountable Talk: Instructional dialogue that builds the mind.* UNESCO. https://unesdoc.unesco.org/ark:/48223/pf0000262675 (accessed 2.12.24)

15 Bennett, T. (2015). 'Consider this a divorce'. *TES*, 5 September 2015.
16 Peal, R. (2012). 'Lies my teacher training taught me #3: most great learning happens in groups'. https://goodbyemisterhunter.wordpress.com/2012/10/24/lies-my-teacher-training-taught-me-3-most-great-learning-happens-in-groups/ (accessed 1.12.24)
17 Howe, C. (2010). *Peer groups and children's development.* Oxford: Blackwell. See also Howe, C., & Zachariou, A. (2019). 'Small-group collaboration and individual knowledge acquisition: The processes of growth during adolescence and early adulthood', *Learning and Instruction*, 60, 263–274.
18 Voice 21 call these productive ground rules 'discussion guidelines'. See https://voice21.org/creating-a-classroom-that-values-every-voice/ (accessed 21.11.14)
19 Rojas-Drummond, S., & Mercer, N. (2004). 'Scaffolding the development of effective collaboration and learning', *International Journal of Educational Research*, 39, 99–111.
20 These and many other student voices have been recorded by Topsy Page in the course of her oracy work. See her excellent book: Page, T. (2024) *100 Ideas for Primary Teachers: Oracy*. London: Bloomsbury.
21 Lovell, O. (n.d.). 'Interthinking: how to make group work, work'. http://www.ollielovell.com/olliesclassroom/interthinking-and-group-work/. Accessed 21.11.24.
22 Student voices recorded by Topsy Page and me.

23 Luckin, R., Baines, E., Cukurova, M., Holmes, W. & Mann, M. (2017). *Solved! Making the case for collaborative problem-solving.* London, Nesta. https://media.nesta.org.uk/documents/solved-making-case-collaborative-problem-solving.pdf (accessed 3.12.24)

24 See Wagner, C. (2023). '"Diminished Voices": Why is it important to focus on oracy when educating girls?', Oracy Cambridge blog, June 7. https://oracycambridge.org/diminished-voices-girls-oracy/ (accessed 2.12.24)

25 'Autistic People Can Work As Part Of A Team', *Different Minds, One Scotland.* Scottish Government, 2024. https://differentminds.scot/lived-experiences/autistic-people-cant-work-as-part-of-a-team/ (accessed 2.12.24). See also *What is groupwork really like*?, Autism & Uni. University College London. https://ucl.autism-uni.org/what-is-group-work-really-like/ (accessed 2.12.24)

26 See, for example, Dong, T., Anderson, R., Kim, I. & Li, Y. (2008). 'Collaborative Reasoning in China and Korea', *Reading Research Quarterly*. 43, 4, pp. 400–24. And Rojas-Drummond, S., Barrera Olmedo, M., Hernández Cruz, I. & Vélez Espinosa, M. (2020). 'Dialogic interactions, co-regulation and the appropriation of text composition abilities in primary school children', *Learning, Culture and Social Interaction*, 24, 100354.

27 'Metacognition and Self-regulated Learning: apply metacognitive strategies in the classroom', *The Education*

Endowment Foundation, October 2021. https://educationendowmentfoundation.org.uk/education-evidence/guidance-reports/metacognition (accessed 2.12.24). See also Chapter 14 of Mercer, N. (2019). *Language and the Joint Creation of Knowledge: The selected works of Neil Mercer.* Abingdon: Routledge.

28 The Thinking Together Project. https://thinkingtogether.educ.cam.ac.uk See also Rojas-Drummond, S., & Mercer, N. (2004). 'Scaffolding the development of effective collaboration and learning', *International Journal of Educational Research*, 39, 99–111.

29 Mercer, N., Wegerif, R. & Dawes, L. (1999). 'Children's talk and the development of reasoning in the classroom', *British Educational Research Journal,* 25, 1, 95–111. Also Chapter 13 of Mercer, N. (2019). *Language and the Joint Creation of Knowledge: The selected works of Neil Mercer.* Abingdon: Routledge.

30 Woolley, A. W., Aggarwal, I. & Malone, T. W. (2015). 'Collective Intelligence and Group Performance', *Current Directions in Psychological Science*, 24(6), 420–424.

31 Vrikki, M., Warwick, P., Vermunt, J. D., Mercer, N., & Van Halem, N. (2017). 'Teacher learning in the context of Lesson Study: A video-based analysis of teacher discussions', *Teaching and Teacher Education*, 61, 211–224.

32 See Chapter 3 of Mercer, N. & Littleton, K. (2007). *Dialogue and the Development of Children's Thinking.* London: Routledge.

7. Teaching and Learning Through Talk

1 Lloyd, C. (2012). 'No Pens Day: The perfect reason to get your class talking'. *Guardian*, 3 October 2012.

2 'State schools should set up debating clubs, says senior Eton leader'. *Guardian*, 16 September 2024. https://amp.theguardian.com/education/2024/sep/16/state-schools-should-set-up-debating-clubs-says-senior-eton-leader (accessed 20.11.24)

3 Goldacre, B. (2013). *Building evidence into education*. A report for the Department of Education. https://www.gov.uk/government/news/building-evidence-into-education (accessed 2.12.24)

4 Howe, C., Hennessy, S., Mercer, N. Vrikki, M. & Wheatley, L. (2019). 'Teacher-student dialogue during classroom teaching: Does it really impact upon student outcomes?', *Journal of the Learning Sciences*, 28 (4–5), 462–512. See also Hennessy, S., Calcagni, E., Leung. A. & Mercer, N. (2021), 'An analysis of the forms of teacher-student dialogue that are most productive for learning', *Language and Education*. DOI: 10.1080/09500782.2021.1956943.

5 I believe this term was first used to describe this way of teaching by Robin Alexander: Alexander, R. J. (2001). *Culture and Pedagogy: International comparisons in primary education*. Oxford: Blackwell. See also Mercer, N., Wegerif,

R. & Major, L. (eds.) (2020). *The Routledge International Handbook of Research on Dialogic Education.* Abingdon: Routledge.

6 All names of students in transcripts have been changed to protect their anonymity.

7 This kind of dialogue also resembles 'Accountable Talk'. Resnick, L., Asterhan, C. & Clarke, S. (2018). *Accountable Talk: Instructional dialogue that builds the mind.* UNESCO. https://unesdoc.unesco.org/ark:/48223/pf0000262675 (accessed 2.12.24)

8 From Mercer, N. (2001). 'Language for teaching a language'. Chapter 15 of C. Candlin & N. Mercer (eds.), *English Language Teaching in its Social Context.* London: Routledge, p. 244.

9 Alexander, R. (2018). 'Developing dialogic teaching: Genesis, process, trial'. *Research Papers in Education*, 33(5), 561–598.

10 *Dialogic teaching – trial.* The Education Endowment Foundation, 2017. https://educationendowmentfoundation.org.uk/projects-and-evaluation/projects/dialogic-teaching (accessed 2.12.24)

11 See Dawes, L. (2012). *Talking Points: Discussion activities in the primary classroom.* Abingdon: Routledge.

12 For more information on these lessons, see Mercer, N., Dawes, L. & Kleine Staarman, J. (2009/2019). 'Dialogic Teaching in the Primary Science Classroom', *Language and Education,* 23, 4, 1–17; and Chapter 11 of Mercer, N.

(2019). *Language and the Joint Creation of Knowledge*. Abingdon: Routledge.

8. Into the Future

1 On Radio 4, BBC science editor David Shukman explained how important it was to meet people in small groups at the 2021 United Nations Climate Change Conference (COP 26). He said: 'It's often in little groups like those when you can take off your masks, that people really get talking about what can be done.'

2 https://gemini.google.com/

3 See, for example, Bob Doyle media: *The Voice Interface of AI*. https://www.youtube.com/watch?v=eGYL94ovTpk

4 See, for example, Elsaspeak. https://elsaspeak.com (accessed 2.12.24)

5 Digitalised Dialogues with Talkwall: supporting classroom dialogue using digital technology. https://digitaledialoger.no (accessed 23.11.24). See also https://www.uv.uio.no/iped/english/research/projects/samtavla/ and https://www.youtube.com/watch?v=80oUi6e4Zbw (accessed 17.12.24)

6 For more on mediation through talk, see Chapters 4 and 5 of Stokoe, E. (2018). *Talk: The science of conversation*. London: Robinson.

Index

INDEX

INDEX

INDEX